LOST IN TRANSITION

LOST IN TRANSITION

The Journey from High School to Higher Education

Kevin S. Koett, Carol J. Christian, and C. Thomas Potter II

ROWMAN & LITTLEFIELD
Lanham • Boulder • New York • London

Published by Rowman & Littlefield
An imprint of The Rowman & Littlefield Publishing Group, Inc.
4501 Forbes Boulevard, Suite 200, Lanham, Maryland 20706
www.rowman.com

Unit A, Whitacre Mews, 26-34 Stannary Street, London SE11 4AB

British Library Cataloguing in Publication Information Available

Library of Congress Cataloging-in-Publication Data

Names: Christian, Carol J., author.
Title: Lost in transition : the journey from high school to higher education / Carol J. Christian,
    Kevin S. Koett, and C. Thomas Potter II.
Description: Lanham : Rowman & Littlefield, [2017] | Includes bibliographical references.
Identifiers: LCCN 2018004589 (print) | LCCN 2018009522 (ebook) | ISBN 9781475842753
    (Electronic) | ISBN 9781475842739 (cloth : alk. paper) | ISBN 9781475842746 (pbk. :
    alk. paper)
Subjects: LCSH: College freshman--United States. | High school graduates--United States.
Classification: LCC LB2343.32 (ebook) | LCC LB2343.32 .C45 2017 (print) | DDC 378.1/
    980973--dc23
LC record available at https://lccn.loc.gov/2018004589

∞ ™ The paper used in this publication meets the minimum requirements
of American National Standard for Information Sciences Permanence of
Paper for Printed Library Materials, ANSI/NISO Z39.48-1992.

Printed in the United States of America

CONTENTS

PREFACE

Colleges and universities across the country begin each fall semester with a new class of bright-eyed, young students who are fresh out of high school with a desire and passion to pursue a career and develop the skills to succeed in a global society. They think they are ready to conquer the world; however, many find they are standing on unstable foundations. Due to anxiety, stress, and uncertainty, many students withdraw before the end of a term, some of whom will never walk through the doors of an institution of higher education again.

The reasons college students withdraw from colleges and universities can be both simple and complex. No matter the reasons, they are legitimate and significantly affect retention and graduation rates. Ultimately, the result is a reduction in the number of individuals equipped with the skills and dispositions to be productive citizens in the workforce and society as a whole.

From juggling personal finances, paying college tuition and fees, establishing effective time management skills, and developing decision making to becoming self-disciplined, some students need support during this transition. High schools and institutions of higher education can enhance student growth by collaborating in the development and implementation of proven transition activities.

First-generation students, students of color, students from poverty, women in STEM, and marginalized students (to name a few) will encounter difficulties during their transition from high school to college. Knowing this, we must ask "What are we doing about it?" Inaction is not a viable option. In doing nothing, many students will become lost in the transition.

Within any given first-year college student, there exists inner conflict. Trying to manage homesickness, independence, making smart choices, self-discipline, peer pressure, and increased academic rigor and finding their niche in a new environment occur while they are making life-long decisions on what they want to do in their careers and as citizens. It makes one wonder how any of us persisted to graduation! As educators, we must work to better understand the developmental and outside influences converging on these young people at a critical time in their development of self.

Abraham Maslow developed what would become the humanistic theory of psychology. Maslow studied the healthier side of human behavior by examining the qualities and characteristics of successful people. The results of his life's work laid the foundation for what is known as a hierarchy of needs. His work theorized that as people's basic needs are met at a given level, they are then enabled to move forward in their development.

Teachers serve in a unique position in watching students grow and many times evolve through these basic needs levels during periods of transition. Educators and parents can work collaboratively to help students during these critical formative years in implementing transition activities. This awareness, combined with transition activities can meet the physiological needs of human beings and catapult them on the journey toward Maslow's highest level of personal growth—self-actualization.

Educators must not lose sight of the basic needs of students as they struggle to grow into fully developed, self-actualized, and productive members of society. Each level of educational transition marks a predominant change in a student's life. Maslow's hierarchy of needs model illustrates how students are launched into action by diverse and often sequential transition events. Factors affecting successful transition for students include the students' self-esteem and self-confidence as well as physical security and academic achievement.

Maslow believed human motivation is based on seeking fulfillment and change through personal growth (Maslow, 1973). Maslow depicts these needs as physiological/basic needs, safety/physical security, belonging/social, esteem/emotional, and self-actualization/completeness. Educators and parents cannot assume that students' needs remain constant as they travel the K–12 system. Life-changing events, such as divorce, displaced families, and changes in family income and student physical and emotional development, affect healthy growth and development, from pre-adolescence through young adulthood (Vitz, 1999). It would behoove educators to implement developmentally appropriate transition plans to better ensure a smooth transition from one school level to another.

Level 1—Basic/Physiological Needs

Level 1 defines the most basic of human needs that are essential to sustain human existence. These needs include oxygen, food, water, shelter, warmth, sleep, and sex. Maslow's theory clearly states that these most basic needs must be met before one can focus on higher needs, such as self-esteem, relationships, or social interaction with peers (McLeod, 2007). Once these needs are met, the individual is then prepared to move to level 2.

In today's schools, as educators are pressured to reach high levels of accountability on state and national standards, the push for improved test scores can cause educators to overlook many of the root causes to low student achievement. Students who sit in classrooms daily who have no safe place to rest their heads at night or enough food in their stomachs to allow them the ability to concentrate are rarely able to perform at their highest levels. If students' basic needs are not being met, schools with high numbers of students of poverty are challenged to meet high levels of academic attainment.

Teachers and school leaders must be vigilant in creating process-es for identifying students whose basic needs are not being met. With systems of support in place to intervene, especially during times of transitions, greater opportunities for success exist.

Level 2—Safety Needs

The second level of humanistic needs encompass safety, security, stability, and natural order (Maslow, 1973). Also included in this level of needs is autonomy from danger, violence, and the fear of threatening events.

As documented in the Statistical Abstract of the United States: 2012, the 1980 United States Census Bureau report found that 85 percent of school-age students came to school from two-parent family homes. Divorce was not as common. Today, nearly one in every four students is being raised by a single parent. Another staggering phenomenon affecting today's students is that one in every fourteen students is being raised by grandparents. In 2010–2011, over a million students were registered as homeless (Homeless Children and Youth, 2015). Many children today leave home never knowing what address they will return home to. Some students leave home each morning, or some semblance of what is called home, only to be alerted over the intercom or with a note from the office as to what bus to get on and where the student is to land that evening. More students than we care to admit are living in far from stable and secure living environments.

In many violent inner-city communities, some students lay their heads down to the sound of gunshots in the streets while their counterparts go to bed mentally reviewing class notes from the previous day's lecture in preparation for the next day's test. Schools expect students to follow order and rules when there is little order and very few rules in some students' lives. Transition plans and courses that teach organization and ordering could perhaps, in some small way, help students in meeting this basic need. Schools that offer transition activities that provide resources for parents/guardians of these identified populations can provide support during times of transition.

During educational transitions, communication between schools often begins to break down. In many schools, little to no communication exists to prepare students for the next level or inform teachers of the level 2 needs of individual students. Without transition plans in place, many students become an educational fatality during these transitional periods. Transition plans that provide time and opportunity for the sending and receiving schools to collaborate better ensure student success. Activities that enable teachers to discuss the specific needs of transitioning students allow educators the opportunity to create a more safe and secure learning environment.

Level 3—Love/Belonging Needs

The third level of needs represents the social needs of the individual and the innate need for affiliation with others (Maslow, 1973). At this level, individuals long for acceptance from family and friends and intimate relationships, and they desire to belong to a group, a team, or an organization (McLeod, 2007). At this level, the need is strong to connect, to have a sense of community in which the individual lives. This level of need tends to emerge during later childhood and the preteen years.

Transition plans that are mindful of students' desires to be connected to a group or an organization intentionally include more ways for students to become involved. At each transition level, competition increases. Many students who were once actively involved at the elementary level find themselves being cut and unable to find their niche. It is here that many students begin to become disconnected from school (Eccles, 2003; Lorain, 2011). This disconnect can begin to affect attendance, grades, and behavior in a negative manner. Transition plans that work to develop multiple opportunities for student engagement and involvement through clubs, intramural activities, and teams could benefit students' human growth and development in nurturing their sense of belonging (Eccles, 2003).

Level 4—Self-Esteem Needs

The fourth level of needs is the development of self-esteem. Having gained the sense of belonging from the previous level, one is now motivated to seek recognition and admiration from others. This developmental stage can be characterized by multiple sources of motivation. As an example, "intrinsic and extrinsic motivation may overlap to some degree, because one may be motivated from both an inside and outside source at the same time" (Jafari, 2013, p. 37). Internal motivation comes from the development of self-respect and achievement. External motivation comes from the social status of the individual, focused attention from peers and coworkers, and personal recognition for achievement within an organization or group (Maslow, 1970). People at this level begin to develop the need to identify their worth as individuals. At this level, they seek the recognition of others, such as colleagues, employers, the community, or even family and friends. The advent of self-esteem typically occurs during the late adolescent stage of development, but for most, it is predominate in adulthood (Maslow, 1970). Once our needs for self-worth and recognition have been met, individuals ascend to the pinnacle of human existence, self-actualization.

Transition plans that provide student recognition opportunities that build confidence can help students during this developmental phase. According to Hertzog and Morgan (1999), teachers and counselors play a critical role in developing transition initiatives that recognize student talents and assist in the development of the adolescent and young adult during the transition from middle school to high school and beyond. Schools must be mindful that such recognition should not be limited to recognizing athletic accomplishments but also include the arts, academics, and vocational talents to name a few.

Level 5—Self-Actualization Needs

Maslow's theory proposes that as people ascend upward, moving from one level of need to the next, they will reach the "apex" of growth and fulfillment, the self-actualization level. Maslow noted the goal of an individual should be to "become everything one is capable of becoming" (Maslow, 1973, p. 163). Self-actualized individuals typically seek truth, wisdom, and meaning in life, enabling them to reach their fullest potential a human beings.

TRANSITION RESEARCH

Life is filled with a variety of transitions. Though the scope and number of transitions we experience in a lifetime are countless, the educational transitions we encounter are critical in ensuring the successful transition of students at each educational juncture.

A transition is defined as the passage from one state, stage, subject, or place to another. Transition can be a movement, a development, or an evolution from one form, stage, or style to another (Hussey & Smith, 2010). Educational transitions can be thought of from an intellectual as well as a physical perspective (Hussey & Smith, 2010). Intellectually, individuals transition from being thoughtless to being thoughtful. At the same time, physical transitions in education involve moving from one building to another or a new environment (Hussey & Smith, 2010).

One of the functions of schooling is to help prepare students to reach their fullest potential as developing human beings. Schools should provide opportunities for students to explore themselves and their talents by creating a safe and orderly learning environment for individual growth to occur. Systemically developed, research-based transition plans at the elementary, middle, high, and postsecondary school levels can better ensure student success during times of transition (Lorain, 2011). Transition plans that include exploratory courses and dual credit opportunities at the high school level, summer transition jump-start programs, and counseling support services are examples of things schools can implement to create a safe learning environment that maximizes learning.

ARTICULATION ACTIVITIES

Though there has been a significant amount of research conducted on the topic of transitions, there is no one path a person can take that will guarantee "success." To promote effectiveness and efficiency during times of transition, schools must include intentionally planned articulation activities. Just and Adams (1997) stated that articulation activities "facilitate a smooth transition" (p. 30). Similarly, Hviid and Zittoun (2008) shared that intentional planned articulation activities enhance the educational process for students in and out of the classroom using trial and error and experimentation as essential components of navigating educational transitions.

DeMott (1999) emphasized being intentional about helping students make successful educational transitions. His work highlights the need to (1) find the leaders and different levels; (2) create and support an articulation committee; (3) determine what should be articulated; (4) draft a scope and sequence paper; (5) review and compare the exit objectives/competencies; (6) adopt courses and adapt programs to ensure success; and (7) review, revise, and update the systems (pp. 47–49).

DeMott attempted to create educational systems that lower student anxiety during educational transitions. If students are anxious about the new environment, the new teachers' expectations, and opportunities for extracurricular involvement and increased academic rigor, then schools should develop transition activities to help alleviate these anxieties.

It is important that effective schools create systemic transition plans to aid students during the various school-level transitions. Anxieties are the same for students at all levels. Students share the same concerns of being able to reach higher academic standards and being comfortable with the new and larger learning environment and the fear of being able to fit in and find their worth. Parents, as well, share many concerns during times of transition that encompass questions on parental involvement at the school, systems of communication from school to home, familiarity with the new surroundings, teacher expectations, and the support systems available to them. Parental concerns can also being addressed through intentionally planned transition articulation activities.

A review of literature is provided on the transition from high school to postsecondary institutions.

HIGH SCHOOL TO POSTSECONDARY SCHOOL TRANSITION

One of the final transitions students face during their educational career is the transition from high school to postsecondary settings. According to Malone (2009), high school students need structured transition activities similar to those necessary for the middle school to high school transition. A quality articulation activity must have (1) a purpose that is easily understood, (2) committed leaders, (3) appropriate financial support, (4) effective collaboration among constituents, (5) a holistic approach, and (6) an emphasis on long-term effect (Malone, 2009).

Malone (2009) provides two examples of articulation activities that demonstrate the aforementioned tenets. Specifically, summer-term programs and intentional activities for students while they are still in high school are outlined as effective articulation activities (Malone, 2009). Both require more than a one-day, hit-or-miss approach to helping students better prepare for the transition from high school to postsecondary institutions.

One example of a summer transition program is a program being implemented at a midsized, four-year public institution in the southern region of the United States. The program is six weeks in length and provides first-year students the opportunity to live on campus and earn up to nine credit hours before the beginning of the fall semester. The program is offered to students at a reduced cost; provides one-on-one interactions with faculty, peers, and staff; and requires participants to engage in meetings with mentors, attend study sessions, and experience campus dining services. Participants experience transitional issues and concerns in a more personalized environment than their peers who will arrive in August.

An example of an intentional activity for high school students is a program sponsored by a community chamber of commerce in a small, southern city in the United States. Members of the chamber of commerce created and implemented a presentation in a local high school that allowed students to interact with individuals from community colleges, traditional colleges, and the military in an effort to learn about educational opportunities after high school graduation.

Alexson and Kemniz (2004) identified (1) structure, (2) study skills, (3) family support, (4) peer support, and (5) interactions with mentors as the basis for effective articulation activities for high school and postsecondary students. They specifically stated that "through formal articulation [activities], transition becomes a reality for students" (Alexson & Kemniz, 2004, p. 20). Common examples of the perspective outlined by Alexson and Kemniz are orientation programs and classes.

Orientation programs are typically one- or two-day sessions that occur in the summer. Students and their families are exposed to an extensive amount of information with their primary goal being the attainment of a course schedule. On the other hand, orientation classes typically occur during the course of an academic semester and meet on a regular basis to educate students about institutional culture, resources, study skills, other matters associated with acclimating to a postsecondary environment.

Walker, Downey, and Cox-Henderson (2010) acknowledged the importance of (1) engagement, (2) sense of belonging, (3) academic success, (4) individual motivation, and (5) personal expectations as an individual makes educational transitions. Specifically, they stress the importance of hands-on experience and collaboration with faculty, peers, and staff (Walker et al., 2010). Examples of this philosophy include involvement with student organizations and community service activities. As a result, it is important to expose students to avenues for becoming involved on campus and off campus early in their postsecondary careers. Articulation activities that involve interacting with and learning from others promote successful transitions.

In the transition from high school to postsecondary institutions, students are equally concerned with their ability to keep up with the academic rigor and the social aspects of fitting in, attaining a sense of belonging, achievement, and respect from peers and others. Through the development of intentional, structured, experiential articulation activities that expose individuals to diverse populations and experiences, educators can best prepare students to successfully transition from high school to postsecondary institutions.

If you are a teacher, parent, or school or university administrator, the authors of this book encourage you to intentionally implement a number of transition activities to better ensure that high school students have a smooth and successful transition to college.

REFERENCES

Alexson, R. G., & Kemniz, C. P. (2004). Curriculum articulation and transitioning student success: Where are we going wrong and what lessons have we learned? *Educational Research, 28*(2), 19–29.

DeMott, J. (1999). Articulation eases stressful school transitions. *Educational Digest, 65*(3), 46–49.

Eccles, J. (2003). Extracurricular activities and adolescent development. *Journal of Social Issues, 59*(4), 865–89.

Hertzog, C. J., & Morgan, P. L. (1997). From middle school to high school: Ease the transition. *Educational Digest, 62*(7), 29–31.

Homeless Children and Youth (2015). *Child Trends Data Bank*, p. 11. Retrieved from https://www.childtrends.org/wp-content/uploads/2015/10/12_Homeless_Childrend_and_Youth.pdf.

Hussey, T., & Smith, P. (2010). Transitions in higher education. *Innovations in Education and Teaching International, 47*(2), 155–64.

Hviid, P., & Zittoun, T. (2008). Editorial introduction: Transitions in the process of education. *European Journal of Psychology of Education, 28*(2), 121–30.

Jafari, S. S. (2013). Finding Drive. *Language Magazine, 13*(2), 36–38.

Just, D. A., & Adams, D. A. (1997). The art of articulation: Connecting the dots. *New Directions for Community Colleges*, Spring 1997(97), 29–39.

Lorain, P. (2011). Transition to middle school: Are swirlies for real? National Education Association. Retrieved from http://www.nea.org/tools/16657.htm.

Malone, H. J. (2009). Build a bridge from high school to college. *Phi Kappa Phi Forum, 89*(3), 23.

Maslow, A. H. (1970). *Motivation and personality*. New York: Harper & Row.

Maslow, A. H. (1973). A theory of human motivation. In R. Lowry (ed.), *Dominance, self-esteem, self-actualization: Germinal papers of A. H. Maslow* (pp. 153–73). Montery, CA: Brooks/Cole Publishing.

McLeod, S. A. (2007). Maslow's hierarchy of needs. Retrieved from http://www. simplypsychology.org/maslow.html.

United States Census Bureau (2012). Statistical abstract of the United States: 2012. Retrieved from https://www2.census.gov/library/publications/2011/compendia/ statab/131ed/2012-statab.pdf.

Vitz, P. C. (1999). Family decline: The findings of social science. *Catholic Education Resource Center*. Retrieved from https://www.catholiceducation.org/en/controversy/ marriage/family-decline-the-findings-of-social-science.html.

Walker, D. A., Downey, P. M., & Cox-Henderson, J. (2010). REAL camp: A school-university collaboration to promote post-secondary educational opportunities among high school students. *The Educational Forum, 74*(4), 297–304.

INTRODUCTION

This book focuses primarily on transitions from high school to institutions of higher education. *Lost in Transition: The Journey from High School to Higher Education* is one in a series of three separate but interrelated books that share scenarios regarding the journey through schooling and the obstacles students face in each transition.

As institutions of higher learning examine retention and graduation rates, it is imperative that they work collaboratively with local, regional, state, and national high schools. A strong network of support between high schools and institutions of higher education is critical for creating effective transition activities for college-bound students. Even for first-generation families with significant spiritual and social capital, there is more that can be done between, within, and among institutions to reduce the negative effects transitions can have on students.

We should not assume students automatically adjust and that transitions are simply a part of life. If that were the case, institutions would not need first-year teacher mentoring programs, first-year seminar classes, or counseling sessions. There would be no significant purpose for financial management courses or intentional opportunities to enhance communication skills. Without these programs and resources to prepare students to be successful in college, work settings, and life, some will simply get by and others will succeed. Some will fail and others will become lost in the transition. This pattern equates to inconsistent and declining retention and graduation rates and, in many cases, financial despair due to significant loan debt.

Developing a system of transitions takes effort from someone like a dean of students, director of housing, or other student affairs professional. Students are no longer coming to campuses solely for the academic rigor. They are trying to evolve into independent, well-rounded, and productive professionals, family members, and citizens.

Being immersed in the total college experience and exposed to the diversity colleges and universities have to offer changes the lens in which these young people view the world. However, in the absence of transition activities, this period of adjustment and independence can be overwhelming and scary. This can be even more true for an introvert, a first-generation student, or a student from poverty or for those who may have wealth but suffer from a form of internal poverty. Regardless, many students are ill prepared for the transition from high school to institutions of higher education.

This work is developed with a twofold premise: that, one, educators and parents understand the role they play in meeting the basic developmental needs of individual students during times of transition and, two, school leaders understand how critically important it is for organizations to create structured transition processes to better ensure student success before, during, and after transitions that support the growth and development of students.

Transition success does not happen by chance. Schools must intentionally develop activities that make it easier for students to have an effective transition experience. As students navigate each move through the K–12 and postsecondary school systems, multiple transitions occur that include but are not limited to moving to different and unfamiliar school buildings and going from self-contained classrooms with one teacher to departmentalized schools with numerous teachers. Most building transitions require a move to larger, more impersonal school environments. During these periods of transition students can become lost in the shuffle as they move through multiple-period days, various teacher routines and expectations, more complex schedules, increased academic rigor, and growth and developmental changes. Each of these transitions can pose barriers to ensuring student success.

Many students who lack the support structures from school and home that help ensure a seamless transition become lost in transition. These students may begin to experience an increase in failing grades and inappropriate behaviors. Because of frustration, fear, and the inability to cope with the stresses, many students increase their risk of becoming a dropout statistic.

The research that served as the foundational structure for this book centers on transition research and Maslow's understanding of human growth and development. The literature support of this research serves to assist educators and parents in understanding why it is important to intervene with a purposeful set of transition plans and activities that are intentionally developed to help students during each move from grade to grade, school to school, or high school to postsecondary school.

This book is both practitioner based and parent friendly. It is written in authentic scenarios that are research based to help combat the barriers associated with the transitional moves high school students entering college may experience. It is a goal of this work and the companion books that school organizations and institutions will work collectively to strategically develop district-wide and inter-agency (high school and college) transition plans to help students with these critical periods.

In understanding human growth and basic levels of human need, educators come to better understand the total child, physically, socially, emotionally, and intellectually. In this era of high-stakes accountability, educators must not lose sight of reaching out to students at a deeper, more basic level than merely teaching content. Educators and parents would serve students well in being reminded of the inner, human developmental needs of our students and what schools can intentionally do to ensure successful transitions by implementing transition activities that prepare them for these moves.

In college, educators often study the theory of learning. It is a goal of these authors that in using real-life stories, the connection can be made in bridging theory with practice while providing suggestions for interventions that can be strategically embedded in individualized transition plans.

I

TOP DOG

*Be it the superstar athlete, class valedictorian, or the general
student who thinks "with rank comes privileges," many individuals leave high school feeling like the "top dog." This could be a
result of messages from family members, teachers, coaches,
peers, community members.*

*Within a few months, a majority of those students learn that
they are truly a "small fish in a big pond" when they begin their
post-secondary education. The sudden change in perceived status could have an impact upon the self-image of a young person.
It takes time for individuals to learn that after high school, hierarchy is truly situational. According to Seth Godin (2008), "it
takes guts to acknowledge that perhaps this time, right now, you
can't lead" (p. 87). Instead of allowing their new environment to
be the source of anxiety, students must learn when to be "top
dog" and when to join the pack as a follower and develop other
talents.*

VIGNETTE

Sitting in a local shop, Ashleigh sips a cup of French vanilla coffee
as tears stream down her face. Has she lost a loved one? Did a long-

term relationship end with a broken heart? No. Ashleigh is so focused on a class project that she does not even notice she is crying.

She is halfway through her first semester as a college student and
is working on an assignment for her freshman communication
course. Each student has been asked to submit a cocurricular tran-
script that can include only her higher education experiences. Her
tears are reflective of the fact that Ashleigh has been staring at a
blank piece of paper for days and cannot come up with anything to
complete the project. As the time draws near for Ashleigh to go to
class, she puts pen to paper and writes "I have done nothing as a
college student, and this assignment has helped me see that I should
stop wasting my parent's money and drop out."

Ashleigh is a young lady who comes from a great family.
Throughout her life, she has been taught the importance of a positive attitude, strong work ethic, and community service by her family, teachers, friends, spiritual community, and mentors. During her
high school career, Ashleigh was voted "most likely to change the
world," and her report cards consistently praised her for her ability
to multitask.

To many, her ability to hold a job; maintain a very respectable
GPA; tutor students who were struggling in math; serve as student
government association president; actively participate in the Big
Brothers/Big Sisters program; spearhead the school's recycling program; write for the school newspaper; and serve as yearbook editor,
student liaison with the local Habitat for Humanity chapter, and as a
regular volunteer with the community Meals on Wheels program is
nothing short of "superhuman."

In her high school, Ashleigh was "queen." This was true on a
figurative and literal basis because she was elected homecoming
queen during her senior year. The vast majority of students, teachers, staff, and administrators in her school knew her by name (an
impressive statement given her high school has over two thousand
students) and respected her opinions. If her school had had a formal
hierarchy, she would have easily been considered one of the "top
dogs."

Given her experiences as a high school student, a reasonable person could assume that she would enter her postsecondary experience with a high level of confidence and self-esteem and need multiple sheets of paper for her cocurricular resume. However, several barriers early in her college career caused her to question herself at a deep level.

Ashleigh was told that she could not serve as a tutor until her second semester because she needs an established college GPA to apply for a position. She found college assignments and expectations to be far more difficult than what she had experienced in high school. Therefore, she spent most of her time in the library or her residence hall studying. These days, she is feeling more like a "court jester" than the "queen" she was just a few months earlier.

With the weight of the world on her shoulders, Ashleigh sits through her communication course, hands in the note she had written in the coffee shop, and walks back to her residence hall in tears. "How will you tell your parents you want to throw in the towel?" a voice echoes in her head. The lack of an answer is the source of her endless tears. She knows they will be so disappointed in her.

As she fumbles for her ID to open the door of her residence hall, Ashleigh hears a voice saying "Ashleigh, are you OK?" Confused, she turns her head to see her RA, Jenny, standing next to her. "Are you OK?" she asks again. Ashleigh cannot respond because she does not know what to say. "Do you have time to talk?" Jenny asks. Ashleigh begins to cry harder and simply nods her head.

As they talked, Jenny soon learned why Ashleigh was feeling "lost" in the new environment in which she found herself. Jenny listened to Ashleigh's story for more than an hour. She then shared with Ashleigh that she had been in the exact same position when she arrived on campus. She too had felt lost and wanted to go home, where she thought she would feel more comfortable. In fact, Jenny shared that when she started college, she was one of those who did in fact go home. Within a few weeks, however, she realized she had made a huge mistake. The next semester, Jenny shared that she returned to school and found one organization that interested her and joined. Now, Jenny is involved with more than ten student organizations and is an RA. She is a leader in some and a regular participant in others but an active member in all of them. Jenny asked Ashleigh to remain on campus and promised to help her become more involved.

To help the situation, Jenny simply invited Ashleigh to join her for lunch for a few weeks. During that time, she introduced her to several of her friends who were involved with countless activities and organizations.

Although Ashleigh took a little time to decide which groups were right for her, she remained focused on her academics, and she no longer feels the need to drop out. She is a regular lunch guest of Jenny and sees those social opportunities as important elements of her college experience. With the guidance of others and opportunities to become involved on campus, Ashleigh's levels of self-esteem and self-image have returned to where they were when she was a high school student.

RESEARCH

As students move from one institution to another, they will experience a variety of changes and transitions. To best prepare, students should understand the possible concerns that might arise before they occur and cause them stress.

Hicks and Heastie (2008) confirm this assessment in their assertion that "during the transition from the high school environment, students often experience personal and emotional problems, global psychological distress, somatic distress, anxiety, low self-esteem, and depression" (p. 143). It is important for students and parents to understand that these feelings are normal and, in a vast majority of cases, temporary.

Similarly, the research of Hair and Graziano (2003) supports the importance of high self-esteem as a means for students to have academic success as they transition from one level of education to another.

The work of Alexander Astin is most applicable to Ashleigh's situation. Astin's studies note the correlation between student involvement and satisfaction with the college experience (Astin & Schroeder, 2003). Had Ashleigh been able to make more immediate connections on campus, she may have avoided the feelings of wanting to drop out.

Smith and Zhang (2009) address concerns associated with the transition from high school to college with regard to academics. Specifically, the authors collected data from students who attended a midsized institution in the southern United States. In their work, Smith and Zhang (2009) reference the fact that students have little knowledge of what they will experience at an institution of higher education. Similarly, the authors note that teachers struggle with mentoring students on how to prepare for college (Smith & Zhang, 2009).

INTERVENTIONS

There are countless Ashleighs in the world. Many students move from a position of being on top of the world in high school to feeling inferior in college. As noted by Astin and Schroeder (2003), the stronger the sense of involvement and connection a student has to an institution, the more likely she will persist to graduation. As a result, it is critical to actively engage students in the college environment as soon as possible.

In addition to the need for timely student engagement, it is important to provide students with resources to help them acclimate to their new environment. As noted by Smith and Zhang (2009) and Michael, Dickson, Ryan, and Koefer (2010), students in transition require strong mentors and resources to help them navigate. Smith and Zhang (2009) also note the important role that parents, educators, and colleagues play in helping students during educational transitions. As a result, it is essential to provide strong educational materials and resources for the best possible influence on the students making educational transitions.

No matter the articulation activities educators implement, Walker, Downey, and Cox-Henderson (2010) state that successful transitions occur when individuals are provided with "hands-on" and "[real] life experiences in a post-secondary setting" (p. 300). Parents, mentors, and high school and postsecondary educators need to focus on helping students actively engage in experiential learning as they make educational transitions.

Strategies and suggestions:

- Create strong orientation programs that educate new students about traditions and matters that are unique to the institution.
- Provide educational materials for students and parents so they have a clear understanding of the issues new students might experience in college and examples of resources that students can use to work through those issues. Resources include housing staff members, admissions counselors, tutors, faculty members, attending open house and orientation programs, and career services professionals.
- Create college transition sessions in high schools where students can hear real-life examples of college transition experiences they will encounter.
- Create strong training programs for housing staff members (to include resident advisors, hall directors, etc.), to identify and address students who might be struggling early in their college careers. Examples include students who are experiencing homesickness, isolation, change in hygiene, being overly emotional, and not going to class.
- Train high school administrators and educators as well as college faculty and staff on how to identify, assist, and properly provide information about students who might be struggling academically. Examples include students who are exhibiting a change in hygiene, not attending class, failing to complete assignments, and not engaged in class.
- Create faculty/staff mentoring programs for students in high school and college. These programs would pair individuals with students in an effort to provide them with information on

what to expect during the transition period from high school to college as well as how to navigate a college environment. Examples include assigning mentors based on intended major, ethnicity, or academic preparedness or on a random basis.

- Create orientation activities that help students with transitional issues. Examples include sessions on time management and taking notes, meeting with upperclass students to talk about lessons they learned during their transition from high school to college, and meeting with housing staff to understand issues associated with living in a community environment.
- Use this example (or others) as a case study to determine how individuals would react and what resources would be available to assist.

REFERENCES

Astin, A. W., & Schroeder, C. (2003). What matters to Alexander Astin? A conversation with higher education's senior scholar. *About Campus, 8*(5), 11–18.

Godin, S. (2008). *Tribes: We need you to lead us.* New York, NY: Portfolio.

Hair, E. C., & Graziano, W. G. (2003). Self-esteem, personality and achievement in high school: A prospective longitudinal study in Texas. *Journal of Personality, 71*(6), 971–94.

Hicks, T., & Heastie, S. (2008). High school to college transition: A profile of the stressors, physical and psychological health issues that affect the first-year on-campus college student. *Journal of Cultural Diversity, 15*(3), 143–47.

Michael, A. E., Dickson, J., Ryan, B., & Koefer, A. (2010). College prep blueprint for bridging and scaffolding incoming freshmen: Practices that work. *College Student Journal, 44*(4), 969–78.

Smith, W. L., & Zhang, P. (2009). Students' perceptions and experiences with key factors during the transition from high school to college. *College Student Journal, 43*(2), 643–57.

Walker, D. A., Downey, P. M., & Cox-Henderson, J. (2010). REAL camp: A school-university collaboration to promote post-secondary educational opportunities among high school students. *The Educational Forum, 74*(4), 297–304.

2

WE'RE NOT IN KANSAS ANYMORE

I was hurt when she sneaked out, returning only to get her clothes while I was not there. I was devastated when the dormitory director told me the girl's parents requested a room change. Being a proper Negro did not shield me from inequality, but failed me.

—Parmer (1994, p. 440)

VIGNETTE

On a hot Saturday in August, Joseph begins his college career dressed in a pair of shorts and a t-shirt with the school logo on it that he bought from the college bookstore earlier in the summer while attending summer orientation. Standing outside his residence hall, he looks up at the six-story building, which to him appears taller than a New York skyscraper. Joseph is simultaneously filled with the excitement that comes with being a new college student and the fear that accompanies being in unfamiliar territory.

After what seemed like a hundred trips up and down the stairs, Joseph begins the process of trying to organize his residence hall room. Though supportive of his decision to attend college, Joseph's parents are like deer in headlights during this journey because neither of them earned a college degree. In fact, his father has an eighth-grade education, and his mother did not finish high school because she was pregnant with Joseph. Their actions make it clear they want to leave as soon as possible because they have always been "out of sight, out of mind" people. The sooner they get home, the more comfortable they will feel.

Like many students, Joseph comes from a very small rural town. His community is filled with hard-working folks, but diversity is limited to whether you wear cowboy boots or work boots out to dinner. Like the endless miles of cornfields, the people in Joseph's hometown all look the same.

Seeing their discomfort, Joseph kisses his mom on the cheek and his dad on the forehead, sending them the message that everything will be alright and it is time for them to depart. With a "good luck" handshake from his father and a "we love you" from his mother, the couple prepare to leave. However, before they can make it out of the room, Joseph's roommate arrives. "Hello, I'm Thomas," he says. Thomas continues, "I am glad to finally meet you," extending his hand to greet Joseph.

While the two roommates greet each other, neither notices the look of horror that has come over Joseph's parents. When Thomas leaves the room to retrieve more of his belongings from his vehicle, Joseph's mother calls the housing office.

"Hello, this is the housing office. How may I help you?" says the director of housing. "My son needs a different room immediately," she says. "Is something wrong with his room?" replies the director. "There most certainly is," states Joseph's mother. "He must be moved immediately." By this time, Joseph has noticed that his mother is on the phone and Thomas has returned with a load of personal belongings.

The director asks for more information about the cause for the room change request. In the softest voice possible, Joseph's mother responds, "His roommate is a Negro." "I'm sorry, but I cannot hear you. Can you please repeat yourself?" the director responds. Still in a voice barely audible, Joseph's mother says, "His roommate is a Negro."

The director repeats himself to share the concern that he cannot hear what she is saying. He continues by asking, "Why are you talking so quietly?" "I am in the room with my son and his roommate," she replies. "Can you please repeat your concern, as I cannot hear what you are saying?" asks the director. Though not yelling, she says in a voice that can be heard in the room, "My son's roommate is a Negro." At that moment, it appeared as if the entire universe went silent and all eyes in the room turned to Joseph's mother.

The director shared with the mother that ethnicity is not a factor used by the housing office to make room changes. However, he assured the mother he would check on the room as soon as possible. When the call ended, Joseph's mother assured her son he would be moved to a new room, and she and her husband departed for their journey home.

After a few minutes of awkward silence, Thomas asked Joseph if he was a racist. "Hell no," said Joseph, somewhat offended by the question. "Then why was your mom calling me a Negro and wanting you to change rooms?" "We just don't see many colored people where I'm from," said Joseph. Thomas quickly responded by saying, "First of all I am black, not colored, and, second, I do not want to live with a racist."

Still trying to figure each other out, the two continued the process of moving their belongings into the room and organizing them. Later in the day, the director of housing stopped by to check in on Thomas and Joseph. After hearing from both students, he asked them to "give things a try for a few days" and then to see if a room change would be necessary.

After about two weeks, Thomas and Joseph went to the housing office together to ask for a room change. The two had no major issues with each other (in fact they had become friends as they learned to know each other a little more); however, they simply could not overcome the events that had occurred on the day they met.

RESEARCH

As with many aspects of life, prior knowledge of an activity or environment can help a person successfully navigate similar events. This concept is especially true when referencing attending an institution of higher education. Individuals who are the first from their families to attend a college or university (first-generation students) are less likely than their counterparts to have a positive experience and persist to graduation (Inkelas, Daver, Vogt, & Leonard, 2007).

The lack of knowledge about colleges and universities is demonstrated by the fact that about only one-third of students who meet the definition of being first generation actually attend a postsecondary institution (Inkelas et al., 2007). As stated by Fischer (2007), this lack of experiential reference is a significant contributor to why the transition from high school to college "can be complex" (p. 128).

In addition to research on first-generation students, Mendoza-Denton, Downey, Davis, Purdie, and Pietrzak (2002) acknowledge the existence of self-esteem issues with students of color as a result of a "history of rejecting behaviors" (p. 896). As a result, insensitive behavior from others could be magnified when directed at minority students.

INTERVENTIONS

Students who attend colleges and universities come from countless backgrounds and have a variety of experiences—some broad and some limited in scope. Schwitzer, Griffin, Ancis, and Thomas (1999) focus on educational transitions for students of color. The authors outline the importance of providing students of color with real-life examples of issues they may experience in a college environment and effective mentors as students transition between educational environments.

Similarly, Baker and Narula (2012) state that building strong connections to an institution, involving families, and implementing a collaborative approach to helping students are essential to promoting successful educational transitions. The following activities can help them better understand the diversity that exists on college and university campuses.

Strategies and suggestions:

- Provide educational materials for students and parents so they have a clear understanding of the diversity that exists at colleges and universities. Smith and Zhang (2009) note the important role parents, educators, and colleagues play in helping students during educational transitions. As a result, it is essential to provide strong educational materials and resources for the best possible influence on the students making educational transitions.
- Provide students and parents with experiential opportunities during open house or orientation programs to exhibit examples of how they might react to a roommate of a different ethnicity or culture. Examples could include interactive role-plays, skits, or panel discussion activities.
- Create a venue for students to learn about the strengths and limitations for social media sites because we live in a society where individuals are prejudged as a result of what is present, or not present, on their social media sites, such as Facebook, Instagram, and Twitter.
- Plan and implement forums that include parents and students discussing real-life scenarios to better educate them and diffuse issues that might arise.
- Train college faculty and staff on how to identify and assist students who might be struggling with cultural diversity.
- Create strong mentoring programs for students of color that include specific learning outcomes for mentors and mentees.
- Intentionally plan separate, nonthreatening events for high school and college students in which they can interact with others. Examples include ice cream socials, club and organization awareness fairs, and campus-wide entertainers/speakers.

- Create specific orientation activities that help students with transitional issues related to diversity. Examples include moving from an urban area to a rural area, moving from a rural area to an urban area, highlighting student clubs and organizations that focus on diversity issues, and sponsoring meet-and-greet social opportunities.
- Use this example (or others) as a case study to determine how individuals would react and what resources would be available to assist.

REFERENCES

Baker, K., & Narula, B. (2012). The connected adolescent: Transitioning to middle school. *Leadership*, *41*(5), 16–20.

Fischer, M. J. (2007). Settling into campus life: Differences by race/ethnicity in college involvement and outcomes. *Journal of Higher Education*, *78*(2), 125–61.

Inkelas, K. K., Daver, Z. E., Vogt, K. E., & Leonard, J. (2007). Living-learning programs and first-generation college students' academic and social transition to college. *Research in Higher Education*, *48*(4), 403–34.

Mendoza-Denton, R., Downey, G., Davis, A., Purdie, V. J., & Pietrzak, J. (2002). Sensitivity to status-based rejection: Implications for African American students' college experience. *Journal of Personality & Social Psychology*, *83*(4), 896–918.

Parmer, T. (1994). I am a t-shirt. *Journal of Counseling & Development*, *72*(4), 440–41.

Schwitzer, A. M., Griffin, O. T., Ancis, J. R., & Thomas, C. R. (1999). Social adjustment experiences of African American college students. *Journal of Counseling and Development*, *77*(2), 189–97.

Smith, W. L., & Zhang, P. (2009). Student's perceptions and experiences with key factors during the transition from high school to college. *College Student Journal*, *43*(2), 643–57.

3

NOT MY BROTHER'S KEEPER

College students' perceptions of drinking norms influence their engagement in binge drinking.

—Seo and Li (2010, p. 263)

VIGNETTE

On September 10, Tammy was awakened by the loud voice of a police officer. "Tammy, it is time for your arraignment. Please come with me," said the officer. What a strange dream she thought. "Tammy, get up. It is time to go," said the officer in a more stern, loud tone. This was not a dream. Tammy soon learned that she was in jail. "But how did I get here?" she asked in protest. "Come with me, please" is all she heard.

The answer to her question could be found in the first month of her college career. By most standards, Tammy was fully prepared to attend college. She was an excellent high school student and scored well on her ACTs. In addition, Tammy came from a family where her parents and two siblings had graduated from college. In short, she was academically prepared and had anecdotal knowledge of what to expect in college from a social and cocurricular perspective.

Tammy demonstrated her preparedness from day one during her college career. She never missed a class, had excellent time management and study skills, and by all measures was on a path to continue her academic success on her way to becoming a lawyer. However, the lure of college social life caught up with Tammy on September 10. She crossed the line and was arrested for public intoxication.

Like many other college students, Tammy enjoyed attending off-campus parties. At first, she attended these events to be with her friends and meet new people. However, that quickly turned into the "work hard, play hard" mentality for Tammy. She was getting her work done and doing well academically. So in her mind, she earned the right to enjoy parties during the week.

Tammy's friend noticed she was "getting out of control" and confronted her on her drinking. "I am concerned about you, Tammy. Every time you drink you get drunk," she said. "College students are supposed to party," declared Tammy. "Besides, it is not affecting my grades, so where is the problem?" Tammy asked.

For two weeks, Tammy's friend had been begging her to stop her reckless behavior. "You are scaring me, Tammy," she shared. "With each new party, you are getting more and more drunk. Please stop," her friend begged. Tammy assured her friend that she was worrying about nothing.

On September 10, Tammy and her friend attended a party together. Because Tammy showed signs of being intoxicated, her friend tried to convince her to leave. "Let's go home, Tammy," she said on several occasions. However, Tammy kept avoiding her friend because she wanted to stay at the party. Several hours passed, and her friend finally convinced Tammy to leave the party. She was highly intoxicated and being very loud as they walked back to Tammy's apartment.

About halfway on their journey home, Tammy sat in the middle of the street and declared that she was not moving until she had another drink. Cars passed her by, and the occupants simply laughed at the drunk girl in the middle of the street. However, her friend did not see the humor in the matter. She was afraid Tammy was going to be injured.

After several attempts, her friend realized that Tammy was not going to move. Having programmed the number for campus police in her phone, Tammy's friend resorted to calling them for assistance. The police responded and arrested Tammy for public intoxication.

RESEARCH

Though they are satirical in nature, society tends to stereotype college students using the lens of the entertainment world with movies like *Animal House* and *American Pie*. Yet there is a reality to the notion that during their transition from high school to college, individuals tend to consume more alcoholic beverages and demonstrate a higher willingness to use drugs, such as marijuana (Fromme, Corbin, & Kruse, 2008).

Similarly, Quinn and Fromme (2011) identify that "alcohol use in the United States is most prevalent during the college years" (p. 1104). Even though there is a significant body of research that identifies the dangers of alcohol abuse, the notion that college is a rite of passage that requires heavy alcohol use appears to be indestructible.

As a result of alcohol use/abuse, students can experience increased risk associated with disciplinary action on behalf of the institution, poor academic performance, sexual assault, and unhealthy behavior to name a few.

INTERVENTIONS

Across the country, alcohol abuse is the primary issue that faces colleges and universities (Saylor, 2011). Baker and Narula (2012) state that building strong connections to an institution, involving families, and implementing a collaborative approach to helping students are essential to promoting successful educational transitions.

These suggestions have particular value when it comes to addressing a topic like alcohol. The following activities are suggestions on how to assist students with the transition from high school to post-secondary education.

Strategies and suggestions:

- Provide educational materials for students and parents so they have a clear understanding of the data associated with alcohol experimentation in college as well as alcohol abuse.
- Create educational sessions related to alcohol and other drugs in high schools where students can hear real-life examples of college experiences and ask questions they might have about the transition.
- Create strong training programs for housing staff members, faculty, and staff on what to look for so they can help identify and address students who might be struggling with addictions or abuse of alcohol early in their college careers.
- Create interactive orientation activities that help students with transitional issues associated with alcohol and social life.
- Provide students with substance abuse/use concerns with educational and recovery opportunties with learning outcomes as opposed to holding them accountable only via sanctions for violating policies.
- Use this example (or others) as a case study to determine how individuals would react and what resources would be available to assist.

REFERENCES

Baker, K., & Narula, B. (2012). The connected adolescent: Transitioning to middle school. *Leadership, 41*(5), 16–20.

Fromme, K., Corbin, W. R., & Kruse, M. I. (2008). Behavioral risks during the transition from high school to college. *Developmental Psychology, 44*(5), 1497–504.

Quinn, P. D., & Fromme, K. (2011). The role of person-environment interactions in increased alcohol use in the transition to college. *Addiction, 106*(6), 1104–13.

Saylor, D. K. (2011). Heavy drinking on college campuses: No reason to change minimum legal drinking age of 21. *Journal of American College Health, 59*(4), 330–33.

Seo, D. C., & Li, K. (2009). Effects of college climate on students' binge drinking:
    Hierarchical generalized linear model. *Annals of Behavioral Medicine, 38*(3),
    262–68.

4

THE "FRESHMAN FIFTEEN" IN REVERSE

If the "Freshman 15" is a real phenomenon, then the first year of college would be a time to focus efforts to encourage healthy lifestyle habits in order to prevent obesity. If, however, the "Freshman 15" is a media myth, then focusing anti-obesity efforts on new college students will prove ineffective and repeated warnings about weight gain may cause unnecessary worry or worsen body image in ways that actually contribute to weight gain.

—Zagorsky and Smith (2011, p. 1389–90)

VIGNETTE

Only the third week of classes, and the entire campus knew Brenda was a cheerleader! Her makeup was perfect and her smile contagious, she had a hair bow for every occasion, and the warm-ups she wore all said "Fantastic Footwork Cheer and Dance." Her energy level was such that her classmates joked that she had a permanent Red Bull buzz. However, truth be told, she never touched the stuff. Brenda was simple a happy person who loved to make others smile.

Sadly, like the effects of Red Bull, people thought she drank to keep such a high. The happiness that beamed from Brenda was short-lived. In less than a week, Brenda's life would change dramatically.

It was the fourth week of the semester, and the cheer squad has been practicing hard in preparation for the first home football game of the season. Brenda and Steve have been partners since the ninth grade, and they want to prove themselves as strong new members of the team. Known for their stunting, the two have been struggling of late. None of their lifts have been working, and the coach is beginning to think they need more practice before he allows them to perform at sporting events.

To make his decision, the coach gives Brenda and Steve a test. If they make two out of three lifts successfully, they will join the competition team. If not, they will be relegated to the practice squad (which in the world of Brenda and Steve is worse than death). The tension in the gym was thick and could have been cut with a knife.

With a few stretches, a cloud of chalk after clapping their hands together, and a loud yell of "Let's do this" from Steve, the couple was ready for attempt one. Brenda went up and right back down. The attempt was a failure. The next two lifts held their fate. Attempt two found Brenda going up strong, and Steve balancing her like he had never done before. As Brenda jumped down from Steve's arms, the two embraced as if they had won Olympic gold medals. But they still needed one more perfect lift.

After a quick drink of water and a few more handfuls of chalk to soak up the sweat on their hands, Brenda was on her way up for their final test. Like the first attempt, Brenda went up without incident but then started to fall. Both cheerleaders dug deep into their souls to find the inner strength to hold on. With a few grunts and screams, the two were able to hold on for a second successful lift. The applause and hugs from their teammates assured the two that they had made the competition squad.

Later in the evening, in a crowd of friends, Steve was overheard saying, "That was tough. I think she's gained the freshman fifteen already." Hearing the roar of laugher, Brenda could only defend herself by saying, "I think you just need a little extra time in the weight room."

Though no one knew how much those words hurt, Brenda took them to heart. She was 5'2" tall and weighed 107 pounds. However, she had never weighed more than 105 pounds before college. "Maybe I have gotten fat," Brenda said to herself. "Maybe I am making it hard on Steve." In a short amount of time, as a result of only a few words, Brenda set her mind to losing some weight to make her a better cheerleader and partner for Steve. With a few less calories during the day and a few more miles on the elliptical, Brenda knew she could drop some pounds.

"It's working," her mind told her. "You're doing great!" The scale read 104. In the days, weeks, and months to come, it kept falling. First 102, then 98, and before she knew it, Brenda weighed 85 pounds. To the outside world, Brenda looked like a walking skeleton. In the mirror, she looked like Ms. America. Though her mind was clouded, Brenda did not feel weak. In fact, the couple hit their moves with the precision of a brain surgeon. They had regained their superstar status in the world of cheer.

Despite her success as a cheerleader, people were worried about Brenda. She was not healthy. Her hair was falling out in clumps, her menstrual cycle had stopped, and she was constantly cold. Seeing the significant changes, the team trainer stepped in and said, "Enough is enough."

The trainer met with Brenda and expressed his concerns. Their session began innocently with the trainer sharing his concerns. "I am worried about you, Brenda; you have lost a significant amount of weight in a short period of time." Brenda shared that she was fine, had not lost very much weight, and that she had a recent physical with her doctor and all was well. Brenda had quickly thrown up walls, and it was obvious to the trainer that he was going to get nowhere with her.

After meeting with his supervisor, the trainer elected to suspend Brenda from practices and performances until she participated in counseling, began to gain some weight, and demonstrated that she could see the concerns others had about her condition. In addition, the trainer met with Brenda's parent to express his concerns and share the rationale for his decision.

From his experiences, the trainer expected the parents to be supportive and work with him to help Brenda regain her health. However, the trainer found himself to be the target of ridicule. Brenda's mother was furious at his allegations and threatened to sue the trainer if he continued to spread "rumors and lies" about Brenda's condition.

In the eyes of her parents, Brenda was beautiful, healthy, and eligible to participate with her teammates. Before the trainer could say another word, Brenda's parents shared that they would not allow their daughter to be treated poorly and that she would be leaving the university. The next day, Brenda withdrew and went home with her parents.

RESEARCH

The work of Childers, Haley, and Jahns (2011) provides significant insight into the need for understanding the reasons students might gain weight as they transition from high school to college. Although colleges and universities are providing students with more nutritional information about the food being served, the reality of college dining facilities is that they are still filled with fried foods, pizza, and items that can be served quickly.

Childers et al. (2011) suggest that peer interactions focused around food and the transition to buffet-style dining both have a significant effect on the typical increase in weight during the freshman year of college. This phenomenon is commonly known as the "freshman fifteen" (p. 306).

INTERVENTIONS

Transitioning from "mom's kitchen" to eating in a college dining facility can be a challenge for students. Not only is the food cooked differently; it can be difficult to obtain accurate nutritional information from a cafeteria environment.

According to Bellmore (2011), articulation activities are most successful when they focus on strong peer relationships and education on new social challenges students will face. Baker and Narula (2012) state that building strong connections to an institution, involving families, and implementing a collaborative approach to helping students are essential to promoting successful educational transitions. The following are suggestions to assist with dining-related transitions.

Strategies and suggestions:

- Provide educational materials for students and parents so they have a clear understanding of the issues they may face with regard to eating in college. Examples include providing sample menus, nutritional information, and discussion questions.
- Create college transition sessions in high schools where students can learn about real-life examples of eating habits of college students. The sessions would occur in high school cafeterias and include a discussion on the differences between high school and college food.
- Create strong training programs for housing staff members (to include resident advisors, hall directors, etc.) to identify and address students who might be struggling with dietary matters. Examples include students experiencing changes in eating habits, body image, weight gain, or weight loss.
- Create orientation activities that help students with transitional issues. Examples include sessions on healthy eating choices, food preparation in residence halls, and effective exercise programs. To some students, eating fast food and not exercising is seen as "normal."
- Use this example (or others) as a case study to determine how individuals would react and what resources would be available to assist.

REFERENCES

Baker, K., & Narula, B. (2012). The connected adolescent: Transitioning to middle school. *Leadership*, *41*(5), 16–20.

Bellmore, A. (2011). Peer rejection and unpopularity: Associations with GPAs across the transition to middle school. *Journal of Educational Psychology*, *103*(2), 282–95.

Childers, C. C., Haley, E., & Jahns, L. (2011). Insights into university freshman weight issues and how they make decisions about eating. *Journal of Consumer Affairs*, *45*(2), 306–28.

Zagorsky, J. L., & Smith, P. K. (2011). The freshman 15: A critical time for obesity intervention or media myth. *Social Science Quarterly*, *92*(5), 1389–407.

5

THERE'S NO SUCH THING
AS A FREE LUNCH

*It is well established in the literature that college students have
poor eating habits and that many barriers exist to achieving
optimal nutrition for this busy population. Little is known about
students' perceptions of this problem or suggestions for improv-
ing their dietary habits.*
—Cousineau, Goldstein, and Franko (2004, p. 79)

VIGNETTE

Imagine your thoughts about what describes an "average college
student." Your mind might paint the picture of a person who did
reasonably well in high school, has career aspirations, or is motivated to have a better life than family members. Similarly, you
might think about a person who lives in a residence hall, participates
in campus organizations and events, enjoys attending parties, and
has more electronic gadgets than can be charged at one time. Although some college students meet those descriptions, Roger has a
different story.

Roger is an African American student who entered college with
unlimited dreams. Both of his parents were teachers, his siblings are

teachers, and he planned on becoming a teacher. From an academic perspective, Roger has been successful. With a 2.8 GPA, Roger meets the requirements set forth by the College of Education teacher education program, and he is on track to graduate on time.

Despite his performance as a student, Roger is struggling. Staff members have noticed that Roger is always in the student center. He is waiting outside the doors when they are opened and the last to leave the building when it closes. The unique aspect of this is that there is no evidence that Roger does anything in the building beyond watching television. Roger does not study, is never seen eating in the cafeteria, and does not appear to utilize other services in the student center (i.e., bookstore, post office, etc.).

Recently, students have been expressing concerns about Roger. Specifically, they have shared that Roger never changes his clothing and he emits a terrible odor. However, the greatest concern is that Roger does not appear to be eating and he has lost a significant amount of weight in a short period of time.

Concerned about the comments being made about Roger, the advisor of a club in which he used to be a member asked Roger whether he would pay him a visit in his office. Reluctantly, Roger agreed to meet with the advisor. After a great deal of silence, the advisor simply said, "You look and smell terrible, Roger. What is going on with you?" Seeing the sincerity in his eyes and hearing the emotion in his voice, Roger began to open up to his former advisor.

Roger shared that the answers to the questions people were asking were quite simple. With the failing economy, Roger's father and mother had both lost their jobs within the past three months. Roger is experiencing feelings of guilt because he is "living the high life" while his family is struggling to survive on a daily basis. As a result of the predicament they are in, Roger has used all his meal plan money to purchase food to send to his family. He eats little to nothing each day and has no money to launder his clothing or purchase personal hygiene items.

Wanting to pursue the matter further, the advisor was disappointed when Roger had reached his limit on the desire to share any more information. Roger thanked the advisor for his time and left the office without another word.

The advisor simply could not watch a young man perish in front of his eyes. Instead, he worked with a colleague, and the two made an anonymous donation of $150 to Roger's meal card. At least he would be able to eat and regain his strength to be able to finish the semester.

Much to the dismay of the advisor, Roger continued to exhibit his usual behaviors. Did he not know about the additional money on his account? If he did, was he too prideful to accept the gift? No. Roger had learned of the anonymous donation and had simply used it to purchase food to send home to his family.

Shortly after using the $150 that had been added to his account, Roger was seen carrying his limited belongings out of his residence hall. Roger had made the decision that he could not continue his education and he needed to return home.

A full year after his departure, Roger was seen on campus again. He had gained weight, but more importantly, he had regained his smile. Seeing Roger in the student center, the advisor rushed toward him to see how he was doing. "How are you, Roger?" asked the advisor. "I have never been better. My parents have new jobs, and I am able to resume my education," he said with a proud grin. "And thanks for the helping hand when I needed it." He had known all along who had made the donation to his meal card. "You're more than welcome young man," replied his advisor.

Roger graduated in December and is now working with at-risk teens to help them graduate from high school and enroll in college. His personal experiences will serve him well.

RESEARCH

As Roger can attest, there are a number of factors that can cause students of color to be less involved on campus and drop out of college at higher rates that their peers (Fischer, 2007). At the same time, Kao and Thompson (2003) state that the income level of par-

ents can significantly affect the persistence rate of students. Eisenbarth (2012) identifies connections between stress and depression;
he exposes the lack of information related to the true connection
between self-esteem, stress, and depression (p. 150).

INTERVENTIONS

In the current economy, college students are being placed in difficult situations that require difficult decisions. Although Roger's experience is extreme, it is by no means unique. According to Walker,
Downey, and Cox-Henderson (2010), successful transitions occur
when individuals are provided with "hands-on" and "[real] life experiences in a post-secondary setting" (p. 300).

Smith and Zhang (2009) also note the important role that parents, educators, and colleagues play in helping students during educational transitions. As a result, it is essential to provide strong
educational materials and resources for the best possible influence
on the students making educational transitions.

Michael, Dickson, Ryan, and Koefer (2010) state the importance
of strong mentoring programs to assist students with educational
transitions. Students need to have individuals upon whom they can
depend to voice their concerns when times are tough.

Strategies and suggestions:

- Create college transition sessions in high schools where students can hear real-life examples of financial decisions they
  will encounter. Examples include proper use of credit cards,
  financial aid, and meal plan money.
- Create case study or role-play scenarios where students are
  faced with financial challenges and required to develop possible solutions to the problems they face.
- Provide incoming students and their families with clear information on options available if they have financial difficulties.
  Examples include availability of student emergency funds,
  ability of financial aid counselors to use "professional judg-

ment" to assist students in need, and community resources that can provide students assistance if necessary.

- Train college faculty and staff on how to identify and assist students who might be struggling on a nonacademic level. Examples include students exhibiting a change in hygiene, not attending class, failing to complete assignments, and who are not engaged in class.
- Create faculty/staff mentoring programs for students in high school and college. These programs would pair individuals with at-risk students in an effort to provide them with information on what to expect during the transition period from high school to college as well as how to navigate a college environment and seek out available resources.
- Use this example (or others) as a case study to determine how individuals would react and what resources would be available to assist.

REFERENCES

Cousineau, T. M., Goldstein, M., & Franko, D. L. (2004). A collaborative approach to nutrition education for college students. *Journal of American College Health, 53*(2), 79–84.

Eisenbarth, C. (2012). Does self-esteem moderate the relations among perceived stress, coping, and depression? *College Student Journal, 46*(1), 149–57.

Fischer, M. J. (2007). Settling into campus life: Difference by race/ethnicity in college involvement and outcomes. *Journal of Higher Education, 78*(2), 125–61.

Kao, G., & Thompson, J. S. (2003). Racial and ethnic stratification in educational achievement and attainment. *Annual Review of Sociology, 29*(1), 417–42.

Michael, A. E., Dickson, J., Ryan, B., & Koefer, A. (2010). College prep blueprint for bridging and scaffolding incoming freshmen: Practices that work. *College Student Journal, 44*(4), 969–78.

Smith, W. L., & Zhang, P. (2009). Students' perceptions and experiences with key factors during the transition from high school to college. *College Student Journal, 43*(2), 643–57.

Walker, D. A., Downey, P. M., & Cox-Henderson, J. (2010). REAL camp: A school-university collaboration to promote post-secondary educational opportunities among high school students. *The Educational Forum, 74*(4), 297–304.

6

IT'S ALL GREEK TO ME

Contrary to the perceptions held by many people in modern society, "Greek letter organizations were founded [on] an appreciation of learning, a commitment to lead, an ethic of service, a love for one's brothers and sisters, and a belief in democratic ideals."

—Jackson and Harless (1997, p. 23)

VIGNETTE

The opening of school is a hectic time for new college students. Questions of intelligence, preparedness, and self-image flood the minds of young men and women as they learn to navigate a new environment. However, Sandra had a significant advantage over her peers. The world of higher education has been a component of her entire life. Her mother has been an English professor for more than twenty years, and her father served as the director of counseling services for fifteen years at a university before his retirement. All totaled, her parents have over forty-three years of experience at institutions of higher education.

In addition, Sandra cannot name a member of her family who does not have some sort of college education. Aunt Ruth is the "outlier" because she has only an associate's degree. On the other hand, her cousin Theresa has set the education pace for the family because she has a juris doctorate and a PhD in sociology. Obtaining a postsecondary degree has never not been an option for Sandra, and she has never questioned her college readiness. She is more concerned about her ability to fit in on a social level.

In addition to being a family committed to academic success, Sandra comes from a long line of fraternity and sorority members. She is confident that she could capture the entire Greek alphabet if she were able to collect the "letter shirts" from her relatives. Though she has heard countless stories about Greek life from her relatives, Sandra is nervous about the recruitment process. What if no one likes her? What if she is not granted a bid? Will she become the "Aunt Ruth" of the family when it comes to being a member of a Greek organization?

On the first day of sorority recruitment, Sandra arrives at the orientation meeting in the student center. Much to her surprise, there were about 150 other students signing up to participate. The perceived pressure from her family coupled with anxiety from the large number of participants in the recruitment process was almost more than Sandra could handle. However, the structure of the meeting provided little time to deal with nervousness. The combination of group sessions, preference parties, submission of forms, and completing bid cards quickly filled her calendar for the first week of school.

It did not take long for Sandra to sour on the entire process. She spent many hours with friends she had met who cried as a result of not "fitting in" with the groups that were their top choices. Some were told they did not have the "right look," others were not strong enough academically, and a few heard "rumors" about what was being said about them behind their backs. It upset Sandra to hear the comments and see them cry. "How can you be part of a process that hurts people's feelings?" Sandra asked herself. How?

Sandra called home one evening and shared her thoughts with a few family members. "I want to drop out," Sandra told them. Having experienced some of the same feelings when they were in college, her family asked her to stick with the process. "It is not as bad as you are being told," they shared with her. "Not everyone is meant to be Greek," she heard in the background. After a long conversation about how she was feeling, Sandra was struck by the overwhelming philosophy that she needed to continue in the recruitment process to maintain family pride and tradition.

Sandra could not remember a time she had been so upset with her family. Pride? Tradition? Not everyone is meant to be Greek? Had her family been accosted by aliens, she asked herself. Sandra simply could not come to terms with why they did not see the process through her eyes. So she locked herself in her room for the evening, reflected on her values, and cried herself to sleep.

Her night was filled with dreams about Greek life. She dreamed of wearing the letters worn by so many of her family members. She dreamed of seeing her friends crying in the background because they did not receive a bid. She dreamed of hugging her mother after accepting a bid and fighting with her after dropping out of the recruitment process. Before her alarm could sound, Sandra awoke to find the bedding disheveled and her heart beating out of her chest.

After showering and getting ready for the day, Sandra was of clear mind about her decision. Today was the day. She was heading to the Greek life office to submit her decision. "Good morning," Sandra heard as she walked through the office door. "How can I help you?" With her head held high, she replied, "I need to remove myself from the sorority recruitment process, please." "I am sorry to hear that. Is everything alright?" said a female voice from behind the counter. "Everything is perfect," said Sandra, "just perfect." She signed the proper forms and left the office.

Though she left the Greek life office with a high level of confidence, Sandra knew she needed to call her mother and break the news. "It's like a bandage, Sandra. Just rip it off and get it over with," she told herself. However, she was not prepared for the pain it would cause.

After sharing her decision, Sandra's mother was furious, not just the "I can't believe you did that" furious. Her mother was the "raise your blood pressure, veins pop out of your neck and forehead" furious. Sandra was thankful the discussion was occurring on the phone. As the conversation ended, Sandra's mother demanded that her daughter return to the Greek life office and rescind her decision. "I will not permit you to drop out, young lady," continued her mother. "If you do, you will be coming home immediately," she said before hanging up the phone.

After getting through the initial shock of the reaction of her mother, Sandra sat at her desk and composed an email that explained her decision in great detail. Within the text of her message, Sandra expressed her love for her family and the power of the lessons she had learned from them over the years. The end of her email simply reminded her mother that she had been taught to respect others and treat them according to the "golden rule." In addition, she shared that "most importantly, you taught me to respect myself. I respect you, Mom, and I respect myself," Sandra acknowledged, "and because of that, I am not going to change my decision."

It is said that time heals all wounds. Though Sandra's mother is still sad that her daughter did not join a sorority, she is proud of the fact that Sandra has found other student organizations on campus. She is doing well academically, engaged in a great amount of community service, and truly enjoying her college experience.

RESEARCH

The messages transitioning students hear about Greek life typically are negative. Although *Animal House* was release in 1978, individuals entering college today are very familiar with the stereotypes the movie portrays. A simple example is that of the "toga party." Immortalized by the film, college students today still use their sheets to create a unique outfit while dancing to "Shout" by Otis Day and the Knights. As noted by Scott-Sheldon, Carey, and Carey (2008), the real and perceived reputations of Greek organizations cause administrators, faculty, and students to question their legitimacy and validity.

In addition to handling the stereotypes of becoming a member of various student organizations, the transition from high school to college typically forces individuals to address the move from dependence to independence. Zirkel (1992) and others state that this transition can be extremely challenging for many students. A significant level of stress develops as individuals navigate the process of learning new skills while remaining true to the desires of their families (Zirkel, 1992).

To the dismay of some parents, the process students use to compare and contrast what is best for their current and future development is highly dependent on the influences surrounding them (Zirkel, 1992). As a result, many students develop their principles and guiding tenets in the absence of their parents.

INTERVENTIONS

Although Sandra is in a unique position with regard to her family, she is not alone in her experiences with recruitment. Many students experience the highs and lows of the recruitment process. Smith and Zhang (2009) also note the important role that parents, educators, and colleagues play in helping students during educational transitions. As a result, it is essential to provide strong educational materials and resources for the best possible influence on the students making educational transitions.

According to Walker, Downey, and Cox-Henderson (2010), successful transitions occur when individuals are provided with "hands-on" and "[real] life experiences in a post-secondary setting" (p. 300).

Jackson and Harless (1997) outline the importance of having a structured model for the implementation of a strong Greek life program. As a result, they created a model that has been implemented successfully at Elon College.

Strategies and suggestions:

- Provide educational materials for students and parents so they have a clear understanding of the issues new students might experience when considering joining a Greek student organization. Examples include creating a "view book" that highlights each Greek student organization, providing recruitment guidelines that are easy to understand, and having a Web page that is easy to navigate to find information.
- Create college transition sessions in high schools where students can hear real-life examples of college transition experiences they will encounter with regard to becoming involved with student organizations.
- Plan and implement programs that allow students to hear real-life examples of the positives and limitations for being involved in student organizations. In addition, have the programs intentionally address what is "fact" and "myth" when it comes to being part of a Greek organization.
- Create unbiased mentors who are available throughout Greek recruitment to help students process concerns or make decisions that are in their best interest.
- Create intentional opportunities for the entire campus community to come together to discuss issues related to Greek life in an environment that promotes honest, open, and productive communication.
- Use this example (or others) as a case study to determine how individuals would react and what resources would be available to assist.

REFERENCES

Jackson, S., & Harless, A. (1997). Returning Greek organizations to their founding principles. *About Campus, 2*(4), 23–26.

Scott-Sheldon, L. A., Carey, K. B., & Carey, M. P. (2008). Health behavior and college students: Does Greek affiliation matter? *Journal of Behavioral Medicine, 31*(1), 61–70.

Smith, W. L., & Zhang, P. (2009). Student's perceptions and experiences with key factors during the transition from high school to college. *College Student Journal, 43*(2), 643–57.

Walker, D. A., Downey, P. M., & Cox-Henderson, J. (2010). REAL camp: A school-university collaboration to promote post-secondary educational opportunities among high school students. *The Educational Forum, 74*(4), 297–304.

Zirkel, S. (1992). Developing independence in a life transition: Investing the self in the concerns of the day. *Journal of Personality & Social Psychology, 62*(3), 506–21.

7

THE LAND OF OPPORTUNITY

For many people, the thought of leaving home and traveling to another country to continue one's education is unfathomable, but for the thousands of foreign exchange students in our country this is a common occurrence. Overcoming the many cultural barriers that these students face is nothing less than heroic.

VIGNETTE

"**A**re you Ms. Smith?" a barely audible voice said coming from the doorway. "I'm sorry, may I help you?" I said after noticing a young Asian woman just outside my office. I had not heard what she said and was a little startled when I looked up from my email and saw her waiting for me. "Please, come in," I said in an assuring voice. "Are you Ms. Jones?" the young woman asked with a volume only slightly higher than before. "Yes, how may I help you?" I said with a smile. "I do not like the food here," she said. "I do not want to pay for the food."

Before we delved too deeply into our conversation, I stopped and asked her to share some information with me. "I know this is a very important issue; first, please tell me your name." "My name is Angela," she said. "Great to meet you, Angela. My name is Pat."

"Where is home for you, Angela?" I inquired. "I am from Japan," she said with confidence and pride. "I have never been to Japan, but it is a destination on my travel wish list. How long have you been in the United States?" I inquired. "About six weeks. I came here two days before school started." "What brought you to this school?" I asked. "I am part of the international student exchange, and I want to be a doctor." "Well, you have made an excellent choice for that career."

"Tell me more about your concerns," I said to Angela. In her soft voice with an Asian accent, she shared her concerns about the food in the dining hall. "There is nothing for me to eat, and I am wasting money by having to purchase a meal plan." "Is there anything you enjoy in the cafeteria?" I asked. "Nothing," said Angela. "I ate there once and was sick for days. I have never been back."

While on the topic of food, Angela took full advantage of her audience of one. She shared that as a result of her experience in the dining hall, she had tried to eat in her residence hall. However, she shared that people steal her food from the common-area refrigerator and it is difficult to find food in the store (as well as expensive when she can find what she needs). "So how are you eating?" "I do not eat very much," shared Angela. "However, I have some Asian friends who live off campus with whom I eat from time to time." Angela shared that she has lost fifteen pounds since coming to campus.

I shared that I was very concerned about her eating habits and would help her in any way possible. I asked whether she had other concerns. After a slight hesitation, Angela shared that she did not feel "at home." She noted that the rules of the university were very confusing and different than her experience with college in Japan. She was not able to smoke nor could she cook in her residence hall room.

She had been through two roommates already and simply wanted to live in a room by herself (which was not possible due to overcrowding in the residence halls). Angela would prefer to live with someone; however, her previous roommates complained that she wanted them to "teach her how to speak better English." To her, the campus was not very friendly, and she spent most of her time alone or with other international students.

In my mind, I was concerned because Angela was discussing areas that should have been covered during the international student orientation. "Did you participate in an orientation process when you arrived on campus?" I asked. Seeing the look of confusion on her face, I asked whether anyone had talked with her about these issues when she first came to campus. "No," she said. "I was simply given the name and phone number of the director of international student support and told to call if I had any questions."

"Was that all?" "Yes, that was it," replied Angela. I assured her we would address the lack of support for international students but that we needed to begin with addressing the reason for her being here—her concerns about meals.

After a long discussion, I was able to provide Angela with resources to address her concerns. She could speak with the director of dining services about her concerns with meals, she was given information on where she could smoke close to campus, and she was put in touch with housing staff in an effort to help with her desire to have a kitchen. Most of all, she was given a listening ear that allowed her to vent her frustrations.

Shortly after our meeting, Angela learned that her grandmother was not well, and she returned to Japan to be with her family. Though I have not heard from her since her departure, I fondly remember her every Christmas as we hang the ornament she gave me as a thank-you gift.

RESEARCH

Although all students experience transitional issues on some level, international students have other barriers to navigate on top of those that traditionally come with educational transitions. As described by Bradley (2000), international students tend to have higher rates of "relationship problems, feelings of isolation, homesickness, academic pressures, finance and accommodation were likely to contribute to difficulties" as compared to other students (p. 425).

Kwon (2009) further explains the importance of creating guidelines and policies that address the concerns of international students in a timely manner. Specifically, Kwon states that institutions that recruit and enroll students from other countries assume a responsibility to identify issues and resources to help address matters as they relate to the non-American students. According to Mathiesen and Lager (2007), failure to do so could result in negative consequences for international students. What might appear to be a minor bump in the road for a traditional student could end the college career of a student from another country.

Concerns with dining services and roommate conflicts, among other things, are seen as rites of passage for a number of college students. However, Dremuk (2012) outlines the need to be intentional when addressing the concerns of international students. He specifically states that "short-term gains from increased recruitment of international students should not and cannot be made at the expense of students and institutional reputation" (p. 11).

Similarly, Aw (2012) summarizes the importance of addressing the needs of international students because "our overall efforts, through cooperative ventures, will be the most important step toward achieving the educational exchange objectives of our universities, our students, and our nation" (p. 11).

INTERVENTIONS

International students experience a great deal of stress during their transition to American institutions of higher education. Smith and Zhang (2009) note the important role that parents, educators, and colleagues play in helping students during educational transitions. As a result, it is essential to provide strong educational materials and resources for the best possible influence on the students making educational transitions.

According to Walker, Downey, and Cox-Henderson (2010), successful transitions occur when individuals are provided with "hands-on" and "[real] life experiences in a post-secondary setting" (p. 300). In addition, Michael, Dickson, Ryan, and Koefer (2010) state the importance of strong mentoring programs to assist students with educational transitions.

Strategies and suggestions:

- Provide educational materials for students and parents so they have a clear understanding of the issues international students might experience in college and examples of resources that students can use to work thorough those issues. It is essential that the information be translated into multiple languages to ensure the information is understandable to multiple populations.
- Engage in focus groups with international students to learn about the issues that caused them the most concern during their transitional period. The information from the focus groups would be utilized to create stronger orientation programs for international students.
- Create faculty/staff mentoring programs for international students. These programs would pair individuals with international students in an effort to provide them with information and skills on how to navigate such things as university guidelines and policies.
- Use this example (or others) as a case study to determine how individuals would react and what resources would be available to assist.

REFERENCES

Aw, F. (2012). The international student question: 45 years later. *Journal of College Admission, Winter 2012*(214), 10–11.

Bradley, G. (2000). Responding effectively to the mental health needs of international students. *Higher Education, 39*(4), 417–33.

Dremuk, R. (2012). Will we be admitting foreign students in 1975? *Journal of College Admission, Winter 2012*(214), 4–11.

Kwon, Y. (2009). Factors affecting international students' transition to higher education institutions in the United States—from the perspective of office of international students. *College Student Journal*, *43*(4), 1020–36.

Mathiesen, S. G., & Lager, P. (2007). A model for developing international student exchanges. *Social Work Education*, *26*(3), 280–91.

Michael, A. E., Dickson, J., Ryan, B., & Koefer, A. (2010). College prep blueprint for bridging and scaffolding incoming freshmen: Practices that work. *College Student Journal*, *44*(4), 969–78.

Smith, W. L., & Zhang, P. (2009). Students' perceptions and experiences with key factors during the transition from high school to college. *College Student Journal*, *43*(2), 643–57.

Walker, D. A., Downey, P. M., & Cox-Henderson, J. (2010). REAL camp: A school-university collaboration to promote post-secondary educational opportunities among high school students. *The Educational Forum*, *74*(4), 297–304.

8

THOSE WHO CAN, DO; THOSE WHO CAN'T, TEACH

The "anyone can do it" theory does ring true, however, to this extent—almost anyone can walk into a room, tell the kids to shut up, hand out some busywork and thereby keep the machinery of schooling moving. But to actually teach—to get kids to transcend themselves, to care about something distant or abstract, to push them to become better than they knew they could be—requires talent and faith and above all persistence.

—Allen (1998, p. 13)

VIGNETTE

In the hot summer heat, Barry is sweating as if he had just completed the New York City Marathon in record time. However, he has never been to New York City. In addition, the last time he ran any distance, he was being chased by a man with a chainsaw on a haunted hayride. He was ten years old at the time. How was he to know the chainsaw and blood that stained it were not real? His friends experienced a bout of laughter that made them struggle for breath, and Barry earned the nickname "Forrest Gump." If he had a nickel for every time he heard "run, Forrest, run," Barry would be a rich man.

What could be the cause of his intense perspiration? Barry and his parents, younger brother, and maternal grandmother had just arrived for his college orientation program. Prior to his arrival on campus, Barry was asked to complete several documents to ensure his day would proceed as smoothly as possible. He was very pleased when his mother asked, "Do you want me to send these in for you?" Like the response from downhill skiers who have been asked whether they would like more snow, the obvious answer from Barry was "Heck yes!"

As is the case with many students transitioning from high school to institutions of higher education, Barry's mother was happy to fulfill her child's request. On the housing form, Barry was listed as a "neat freak." Although he does not know the definition of a clean room, Barry's mother hoped her "little white lie" would result in the assignment of a roommate who would help Barry with his lack of cleanliness. Similarly, Barry's mother listed his intended major as "prelaw" on the orientation data form. She would soon learn her response to that question was also a "lie."

Why was Barry sweating? Yes, the 92 degree temperature was playing a role in his excessive perspiration. However, the unavoidable confrontation that was about to occur with his family was causing his great anxiety, which displayed itself through his sweat glands. Barry is well aware of the expectation for him to become a lawyer. Yet Barry has no desire to study law. He wants to be a teacher and knows that will not be a popular opinion with his family.

Barry comes from a family of lawyers. His father, mother, two older siblings, both grandfathers, and six extended family members are current or former lawyers. In addition, his younger brother plans to pursue a law degree. A teacher in this family would be comparable to being the lone Democrat in a family of Republicans. However, Barry's passion for teaching is strong. Although he has an unmovable appreciation, love, and respect for his family, his desire to be a teacher is just as strong.

Outside of his family, Barry cannot think about one lawyer who has had an effect on his life. However, in a matter of minutes, he can share several teachers who changed his life.

Mr. Smith taught him to understand algebra in one session after so many others had tried and failed. Ms. Jones's class instilled in him a passion for literature when the mere thought of reading a classic novel made him ill only a year earlier. Mr. Thomas helped him appreciate that home economics was not just a class for girls. He is now the primary chef in charge of Thanksgiving dinners at his house. Coach Adams forced him to understand that the lessons in a game that was lost were just as valuable as those that came from a win. His list of examples could continue for hours.

Soon, Barry found himself waiting in a large auditorium with his family. In a monotone voice, the staff member started to rattle off majors, and students began leaving the room to work with advisors on their schedules. Then came the moment of truth for Barry; he heard the announcement loud and clear—"Prelaw." Smiling in his direction, his family knew it was time for Barry to leave. However, he did not budge. Confused by his lack of action, his parents simply stared at him but said nothing so as not to cause a commotion.

"Education," said the voice from the stage. At that moment, Barry stood up and walked proudly toward the exit. His only words to his family were "I will explain later." Though he knew it would be a difficult discussion, Barry had broken the invisible barrier in his life. He wanted to be a teacher, and he was not going to allow the expectations of his family to deter him from his goals.

RESEARCH

The adage that "those who can, do; and those who can't, teach" is nothing less than an insult to the countless professionals who commit their lives to the development and growth of others. Teachers matter. Strunk, Weinstein, Makkonen, and Furedi (2012) state that teachers are the most important school-based influence on student achievement and research suggests that having a particularly good teacher will positively affect students' current academic performance and their future success.

INTERVENTIONS

The reaction a parent might have to a child going off to college cannot be predicted with any level of accuracy. Some parents are thrilled, others are devastated, and some fall at all points in between those extremes. Smith and Zhang (2009) note the important role that parents, educators, and colleagues play in helping students during educational transitions. As a result, it is essential to provide strong educational materials and resources for the best possible influence on the students making educational transitions.

Gniewosz, Eccles, and Noack (2012) discuss the connections between self confidence and transitions. Based upon their findings, the authors highlight the importance of individuals participating in self-assessment activities to promote successful transitions. Although not always popular, students need to determine their own plan for success during their college experience.

Strategies and suggestions:

- Create intentional opportunities for students to be away from their parents and make decisions (no matter how small) without having to rely on Mom and Dad. This will allow students who might disagree with their parents to assert a certain level of autonomy.
- Plan and implement intentional orientation programs to provide parents with information and resources they will need to handle their transition period.
- Create opportunities for students to participate in interest inventories on a regular basis to ensure they feel comfortable with their educational choices (i.e., major).
- Sponsor panel discussions with parents and students to address real-life issues they will face during the transition peri-

od. Also, provide examples of solutions and resources that could be used to address a concern if it arises.

- Use this example (or others) as a case study to determine how individuals would react and what resources would be available to assist.

REFERENCES

Allen, J. L., Jr. (1998). Best education policy is respecting teachers. *National Catholic Reporter, 34*(21), 13.

Gniewosz, B., Eccles, J. S., & Noack, P. (2012). Secondary school transition and the use of different sources of information for the construction of the academic self-concept. *Social Development, 21*(3), 537–57.

Smith, W. L., & Zhang, P. (2009). Students' perceptions and experiences with key factors during the transition from high school to college. *College Student Journal, 43*(2), 643–57.

Strunk, K. O., Weinstein, T., Makkonen, R., & Furedi, D. (2012). Lessons learned: Three lessons emerge from Los Angeles Unified School District's implementation of a new system for teacher evaluation, growth, and development. *Phi Delta Kappan, 94*(3), 47–51.

9

I SING; THEREFORE, I AM

You know them well . . . the countless students who are quiet and reserved, but if they were to come out of their shells they would be positive change agents in the world. Research demonstrates that students who embrace the risks of being involved on campus persist to graduation at rates higher than other students.
—Morrow and Ackermann (2012, p. 483)

VIGNETTE

Reed is a "typical" young man in most senses of the word. He was an above-average high school student but not overly intelligent. As a member of the football team, Reed was there only for his weight and not his athletic ability. He was a good person who had many acquaintances who liked him but very few close friends who knew him. Reed comes from a nice family, which includes a mother, father, sister, and brother who love him. If he were a point on a bell curve, Reed would be somewhere in the middle 68 percent of the population his age.

Like so many of his counterparts, Reed was both nervous and excited about the next journey in his life—going to college. With the exception of attending one 4-H overnight camp as a child, Reed had never slept outside of his own bed. He was raised in a small town, and as a result, his exposure to diversity was limited. Naturally, he was apprehensive about what was ahead. At the same time, he enjoyed his visits to campus and summer orientation program. He had met some friendly students, faculty, and staff during those visits, so he was excited about joining them on campus.

Like his experience in high school, Reed began his college career in an average fashion. He attended some events but spent most of his time in his residence hall room. That all changed when Reed saw a sign announcing that the university was sponsoring a singing competition similar to *American Idol*. To this day, Reed does not know what motivated him to sign up; all he knew was that his church had taught him a passion for singing.

For the first phase of the competition, Reed had to audition to determine whether he would be one of the top acts. Although he sang from his heart, he did not leave the audition with confidence. He reflected that his performance was good but nothing that blew the judges away. For the next three days, Reed obsessed about the competition. Had he been good enough? His journey to the student center on "decision day" was worth the wait. Reed had made it as a finalist.

On the day of the competition, the auditorium was packed, and Reed's nerves were almost uncontrollable. What have I done, he asked himself. What have I done? His nervousness was compounded as his family and a news reporter from his hometown were in the audience to see him perform. They had faith in Reed, but he was not as confident.

The time had come. His name was announced, and the curtains opened. The crowd was even larger than he had imagined. Standing beside the microphone waiting for his music to begin, Reed looked like a watermelon next to a pencil. Standing about 5'5" tall and weighing about 350 pounds, he had a unique body shape. The delay in starting his music did not help because he began to hear people snickering as he stood alone in silence in his rented tuxedo.

Finally, the sound technician was able to start his CD. The crowd hushed, and much to their surprise, they heard a rendition of

"Amazing Grace" like no other. His voice was angelic. After a few seconds of processing their awe, the crowd erupted in a huge round of applause. Reed was a hit with the crowd, but would he make it to the finals of the competition? The judges agreed with the crowd, and he was selected as one of the three final contestants.

For his encore performance, Reed sang "Swing Low, Sweet Chariot," and this performance was even better than his first. The crowd rewarded him with a standing ovation. After all was said and done, Reed was holding the $500 check that was presented to him as the winner of the competition.

RESEARCH

As stated by Morrow and Ackermann (2012), there is a significant connection between student performance and happiness and a "sense of belonging" (p. 484). Though students' experiences are unique, those who become involved in campus life and feel comfortable with the college environment tend to persist to graduation at high rates.

Hausmann, Schofield, and Woods (2007) note that when students lack feelings of connectedness, there may be "important negative consequences" (p. 804). The authors also reference the work of Vince Tinto by stating that a sense of belonging is a significant indicator in whether an individual will remain a student at a given institution.

Pittman and Richmond (2008) take the sense of connectedness a step further by addressing the subject from a more universal perspective. The authors state that students who have strong connections to society outside of the college (i.e., local, regional, national) experience more successful transitions.

No matter whether it be on a petite or grand scale, the sense of belonging students have is an important factor in their ability to navigate educational transitions in an effect manner.

INTERVENTIONS

If left to their own devices, students tend to forget about the importance of developing a sense of belonging early on in their careers. Gniewosz, Eccles, and Noack (2012) discuss the connections between self confidence and transitions. Based upon their findings, the authors highlight the importance of individuals participating in self-assessment activities to promote successful transitions.

Michael, Dickson, Ryan, and Koefer (2010) state the importance of strong mentoring programs to assist students with educational transitions.

Strategies and suggestions:

- Institutions should implement orientation programs that place an emphasis on educating students about traditions and school spirit.
- Faculty and staff members should take advantage of opportunities to have students complete interest surveys early in their college careers to promote involvement in campus activities and organizations.
- When possible, students should be praised for their work. The world is filled with negativity, and a simple kind word may be the spark that ignites the internal flame of passion within a student.
- Residence hall staff should be trained to engage students in meaningful conversations to help them identify ways to become, and remain, connected to the institution.
- Use this example (or others) as a case study to determine how individuals would react and what resources would be available to assist.

REFERENCES

Gniewosz, B., Eccles, J. S., & Noack, P. (2012). Secondary school transition and the use of different sources of information for the construction of the academic self-concept. *Social Development, 21*(3), 537–57.

Hausmann, L., Schofield, J., & Woods, R. (2007). Sense of belonging as a predictor of intentions to persist among African American and white first-year college students. *Research in Higher Education, 50*(7), 649–69.

Michael, A. E., Dickson, J., Ryan, B., & Koefer, A. (2010). College prep blueprint for bridging and scaffolding incoming freshmen: Practices that work. *College Student Journal, 44*(4), 969–78.

Morrow, J. A., & Ackermann, M. E. (2012). Intention to persist and retention of first-year students: The importance of motivation and sense of belonging. *College Student Journal, 46*(3), 483–91.

Pittman, L. D., & Richmond, A. (2008). University belonging, friendship quality, and psychological adjustment during the transition to college. *Journal of Experimental Education, 76*(4), 343–62.

10

WHAT'S WRONG WITH
A MOBILE HOME?

A Latin Proverb states that a person makes his home where the living is best. For some, home is a castle, igloo, nursing home, prison cell, residence hall room, or spacious mansion. On the other hand, some individuals struggle to define the place they call home. Our physiological needs are inherent; however, our definitions on how those needs are met differ from person to person.

VIGNETTE

On college campuses, and in many communities across the country, it is common for people to live in mobile homes. When exploring options for housing, mobile homes can provide individuals with lower-cost options compared to traditional houses. As a result, no one has questioned Todd's living arrangements. He lives in a mobile home.

By most measures, Todd is an average young man who has handled adversity in an above-average fashion. The only child of two loving parents, Todd always had enough of what he needed to get by in life. His family was lower middle class; however, they were rich with love, support, encouragement, and compassion for others.

One day, while sitting in his high school math class, Todd was called to the office. When he arrived, he knew something was wrong because his minister was waiting with the principal, his guidance counselor, and a police officer. Though he still has trouble remembering exactly what happened in the meeting, Todd remembers the words "We are terribly sorry to tell you . . ." What he was told is that shortly after they dropped him off at school, his parents were killed in a car accident.

During the next several weeks and months, Todd was faced with many situations a seventeen-year-old should never have to address—making funeral arrangements for his parents, selling a house, and countless other interactions with people he had never met. After the initial shock, cycle of grief, and bouts of depression, Todd developed a sense of resolve beyond his years. His mission in life became to honor the memory of his parents and to make them proud.

Less than a year after the tragedy, Todd began his college career. Like so many of his peers, he moved into his residence hall and met his new roommate. He also was diligent about attending classes while balancing an interest in social activities. However, about six weeks into the semester, Todd began to struggle with his living arrangements. He began to feel anxious in his room, and the grief over his parents was starting to resurface. As a result, Todd checked out of his residence hall and shared with others that he was moving into a mobile home near campus.

Technically, he was not being dishonest with anyone. His home was in fact mobile. By traditional standards, a mobile home is defined as "a dwelling structure built on a steel chassis and fitted with wheels that is intended to be hauled to a usually permanent site" (Merriam-Webster Online Dictionary: https://www.merriam-webster.com/dictionary/mobile%20home).

However, Todd's "mobile home" was his 1976 Chevrolet Impala. The vehicle was spacious compared to most current car models, had ample space in the trunk to store his limited belongings, and provided Todd with a sense of connection to his parents because it was their gift to him the day he earned his driver's license.

Todd gave it the old college try for a few weeks; however, he soon began giving clues that all was not right in his world. Living in his car was bearable in September; however, October brought with it too many cold nights and gas bills that he could not manage. His personal hygiene began to suffer because he found it difficult to shower on a regular basis without getting "caught." He also had limited access and funding to launder his clothing properly.

Noticing the changes in his appearance and academic performance, Todd's instructors began questioning him about what was wrong. He simply responded with a terse "I'm fine" and ended all conversations about his current circumstances. Eventually, Todd elected to simply withdraw and end his educational pursuits.

Todd has not maintained any form of communication with his friends, peers, or instructors. From time to time, people will catch a glimpse of a bearded man driving a 1976 Chevrolet Impala through the neighborhood; however, the mobile home never sits still long enough for anyone to check to see how he is doing or how they can help him.

RESEARCH

Abraham Maslow is well-known for his work referred to as a hierarchy of needs. Rowan (2007) states that the work of Maslow can be summarized as describing personal development as a series of incremental stages of growth. However, Rowan adeptly notes that the manner in which issues are addressed in the world tends to be uniform. Specifically, the author asserts that we "[treat] everything on the same level" (p. 73).

Such is the case with Todd. It can be, and has been, argued that the manner in which he has dealt with transitions has not been effective. Minogue (2012) states that when people demonstrate "individualism," they are often portrayed as deviant or negligent (p.

257). In his mind, Todd simply identified an issue in his life and addressed it the best way he knew how.

INTERVENTIONS

Todd is simply one of countless students who have baggage that can affect their ability to cope with transitions.

Strategies and suggestions:

- Institutions should create and implement strong lines of communication in an effort to assist students like Todd who have special circumstances. This would allow the school to which the student is transitioning to be prepared to help if, when, or before concerns surface.
- University employees should be trained on whom they should contact to refer a student who might exhibit concerning behavior.
- Residence hall staff should be trained to better ascertain why students are checking out of residence halls.
- Intentional support programs should be in place to assist roommates of people like Todd to help them handle concerns that might arise if they are overwhelmed by an issue (e.g., living with a student whose parents were recently killed).
- Use this example (or others) as a case study to determine how individuals would react and what resources would be available to assist.

REFERENCES

Minogue, K. (2012). Individualism and its contemporary fate. *Independent Review*, *17*(2), 257–69.

Mobile home (n.d.). In *Merriam-Webster Dictionary online*. Retrieved from https://www.merriam-webster.com/dictionary/mobile%20home.

Rowan, J. (2007). On leaving flatland and honoring Maslow. *The Humanistic Psychologist*, *35*(1), 73–79.

11

DON'T JUDGE A BOOK BY ITS COVER

Pretty enough to be a model? Strong enough to be a construction worker? Fast enough to be a professional athlete? Smart enough to be a rocket scientist? Charismatic enough to be a politician? Through media and personal conversations, people spend a significant amount of time placing judgment (positive and negative) upon others. We might be better served if we view the world through the lens of possibilities as opposed to the lens of predictability.

VIGNETTE

Jim is a young man who is bound for success by most standards. His was an organized person who was able to manage a significant amount of responsibility in high school. Manager for the football team, president of the student boosters, member of the Habitat for Humanity Club, and consistent member of the honor role, Jim was able to multitask with a high level of efficiency and effectiveness.

When he enrolled in college, Jim did not anticipate that anything would change for him. He envisioned that he would be highly involved on campus while maintaining academic excellence. He had never experienced anything different. As a result, it was a shock to his system when he was not selected for a leadership position in the housing office. He was devastated. "How could this be possible?" Jim asked himself on several occasions.

About a week after receiving notification that he was not selected for a position, the director of housing called Jim into his office. At that time, the director explained to Jim that everyone on the selection committee agreed he had potential; however, he simply needed a little more experience before being offered the position for which he applied. Still confused, Jim listened intently.

The director went on to share with Jim that he would like him to consider participating in a different opportunity within housing. "We need strong voices in housing to represent the opinions of other students," he shared with Jim. "We think you would be incredible in this role, and it would allow you to grow and develop skills that will help when you reapply for the other position next year," the director elaborated.

Stunned at first, Jim allowed the words of the director to sink in. "You think I have potential?" Jim offered in a rhetorical question. "You want me to be a voice for others?" he continued. "Yes," the director offered. "This will allow you to assume a leadership position and work toward your ultimate goal." "I'll do it," Jim replied with a huge smile and a great sense of pride.

For the remainder of his first year, Jim was highly successful in his role. He gained the confidence of his peers and served as an excellent representative on their behalf. As he was preparing to leave for the summer, the director of housing called Jim to offer him the position for which he had been denied less than a year prior. After a short hesitation, Jim shared that he appreciated the offer but he preferred to remain in his current position. He was happy with his role and had three more years in front of him if he wanted to reapply for the other opportunity.

RESEARCH

Astin, Astin, Chopp, DelBanco, and Speers (2007) provide a strong foundational framework for helping students be successful in college. Many students leave high school with an image of what being a college student will entail. For many, those notions turn out to be false, yet they exist until they are disproven.

Astin et al. (2007) state that all students must come to terms with who they are by answering a series of thought-provoking questions. However, individuals often do not have the skill sets to effectively engage in true self-reflection. As a result, university personnel have a unique opportunity to help individuals by having open, honest dialogue when timely and appropriate to assist students.

Tinto (2009) states that students require open and honest dialogue to feel a sense of connection and value in their college experiences. It is easy to send a student applicant a rejection letter. However, it is more effective if higher education professionals take the time to share the potential a student has to be successful during a conversation as to why he or she may not have been selected for a specific opportunity.

INTERVENTIONS

The need to work has become a reality for many college students. As a result, it is critical that appropriate interventions be implemented to help students grow and develop in a manner that will assist them with the transitions they face in college. Gniewosz, Eccles, and Noack (2012) discuss the connections between self confidence and transitions. Based upon their findings, the authors highlight the importance of individuals participating in self-assessment activities to promote successful transitions.

Hertzog and Morgan (1998) identify the need to establish "transition [teams]," which create a broad collaboration to assist students with acclimation to a new environment (p. 94).

Strategies and suggestions:

- Institutions should create protocols where decisions about such things as employment are communicated in person as opposed to via letter or email. Such a program would allow for meaningful conversations and growth.
- Colleges should provide students with opportunities to complete interest inventories to explore ideas in a nonthreatening environment, such as the career services office.
- Enrollment services offices should intentionally collect data about student interests in high school in an effort to help make similar connections in college and affect transitional issues in a positive manner.
- Use this example (or others) as a case study to determine how individuals would react and what resources would be available to assist.

REFERENCES

Astin, A. W., Astin, H. S., Chopp, R., Delbanco, A., & Speers, S. (2007). A forum on helping students engage the "big questions." *Liberal Education, 93*(2), 28–33.

Gniewosz, B., Eccles, J. S., & Noack, P. (2012). Secondary school transition and the use of different sources of information for the construction of the academic self-concept. *Social Development, 21*(3), 537–57.

Hertzog, C. J., & Morgan, P. L. (1998). Breaking the barriers between middle school and high school: Developing a transition team for student success. *NASSP Bulletin, 82*(597), 94–98.

Tinto, V. (2009). How to help students stay and succeed. *Chronicle of Higher Education, 55*(22), A33.

12

THE DOG DAYS OF COLLEGE

Imagine being blind and attempting to navigate the stressors of college life. Many students without disabilities struggle with academic, social, emotional, and physical adjustments that occur during their college careers. As one might predict, the educational transitions for the visually impaired are magnified as compared to their peers without sight concerns.

VIGNETTE

In her second week of college, Sam finds herself so exhausted that she has slept through her alarm clock. Without a roommate to holler at her to wake up, the alarm sounds without attention. Instead, Sam continues to dream about being at the beach with the sun hitting her back and water splashing her face. She soon is wide awake with the realization that her face is wet as a result of a tongue bath from her dog and not the salty waves of the ocean.

Sam does not attend a college that allows pets. Instead, she lives with a service animal named Tiger. As a blind student, Sam relies heavily on Tiger to assist her with her daily activities (although it appears Tiger overslept as well). Though frustrated with herself, Sam is very forgiving of Tiger because she has only been with her for less than a week. Fresh out of her extensive training, Sam will cut her a little slack this time.

Over the course of the semester, Sam and Tiger experience their share of problems. Although Tiger is never in public without her blaze-orange vest informing people she is on duty, students, faculty, and staff have had difficulty adjusting to a dog being on campus. Sam is often late to class. Individuals stop her on a regular basis and attempt to pet or play with Tiger. Politely, Sam has to explain that Tiger cannot "play" when she is wearing her vest. On other occasions, Sam has had to deal with students trying to feed Tiger. Similar to her strict work ethic, Tiger is also on a regimented diet for her to be the best assistant she can be for Sam.

Though she has handled herself in a gracious and courteous manner, Sam has reached her limits. As a result, she meets with the coordinator of student advocacy to share her concerns. "I just want to get my education without being afraid of how people are treating Tiger," Sam shared with conviction. She is afraid that Tiger is too young to maintain her sense of discipline and that they both will be placed in danger if that occurs.

After brainstorming ideas to address Sam's concerns for almost an hour, the coordinator asks whether Sam would be willing to "go public" with her concerns. Not knowing his definition of "public," Sam asks for clarification. The staff member asks whether she would be willing to participate in an interview with the college's radio station to enhance awareness about the special nature of service animals.

After a short time of consideration, Sam agrees. Though frustrated by what she and Tiger have endured, she is confident that the actions of others have been out of ignorance as opposed to malice. Together, she is confident that she and the coordinator can help educate the campus about Tiger and service animals in general.

Two weeks after their initial meeting, Sam and the coordinator went on air and spoke about proper etiquette with regard to service animals. It will take time to determine whether the interview will have a significant effect on the behavior of others. However, in the short-term, Sam has found that people have begun to respect Tiger more and appreciate that she is working to help Sam. In turn, Sam has worked with the coordinator to have times when Tiger is off duty and can interact with others. Tiger seems to appreciate fewer distractions when she is on duty and loves the attention when she is not working.

RESEARCH

For many people, the thought of having the person they love the most being mistreated is concerning. Kwong and Bartholomew (2011) suggest the same is true of the bond between owners and service animals. When given significant thought, it makes sense.

A person with a service animal is placing her safety in the control of an animal that cannot communicate with her in a direct and clear manner. Bedwell-Wilson (2009) confirms the notion because she states that the primary role service animals provide in the lives of their owners is preventing them from harm. Some will argue that such a relationship defines trust at the highest level. As a result, owners of service animals experience significant levels of frustration and grief when their companions are mistreated or they pass away (Kwong & Bartholomew, 2011).

In addition to preventing harm, Shaughnessy (2008) learns in an interview with Melissa Winkle that service animals create feelings of security for their owners by serving as "social conduits" and unconditional "companionship" (p. 35).

The effective training of a service animal and matching it with a proper owner can provide a person with a disability opportunities that allow him or her to pursue dreams and opportunities that would not otherwise be possible.

INTERVENTIONS

Sam is a young woman who simply wants to pursue her dream of being a college graduate. Without the help of Tiger, her passion would have gone unfulfilled.

Malone (2009) identifies the importance of summer transition programs and the role they play in assisting students. Sam and other students can benefit from summer programs to help with acclimation and transition issues.

Hertzog and Morgan (1998) identify the need to establish "transition [teams]," which create a broad collaboration to assist students with acclimation to a new environment (p. 94).

According to Walker, Downey, and Cox-Henderson (2010), successful transitions occur when individuals are provided with "hands-on" and "[real] life experiences in a post-secondary setting" (p. 300).

Strategies and suggestions:

- Educators and educational administrators should create open lines of communication, which allow students with disabilities to transition from one institution type to another without incident.
- Postsecondary institutions should create summer programs that allow students with disabilities to explore the campus, residence halls, and academic buildings at their leisure prior to their first semester of enrollment.
- The campus disabilities services coordinator should communicate with appropriate institutional personnel to ensure they are aware of the accommodations to which a student with disabilities is entitled well in advance of his or her arrival so they can be in place from the beginning of the student's career.
- Appropriate campus personnel should meet with students with disabilities on an individual basis to determine what they are comfortable sharing (if anything) about their service animals. If the owner is comfortable, the institution should use avail-

able avenues to educate the general campus population about the dos and don'ts of interacting with service animals.

- If the student is comfortable, he or she could schedule times when members of the campus community could interact with the service animal in an effort to remove the novelty of having an animal on campus.
- Use this example (or others) as a case study to determine how individuals would react and what resources would be available to assist.

REFERENCES

Bedwell-Wilson, W. (2009). Constant companions. *Dog World*, *94*(12), 20–22, 25, 36.

Hertzog, C. J., & Morgan, P. L. (1998). Breaking the barriers between middle school and high school: Developing a transition team for student success. *NASSP Bulletin*, *82*(597), 94–98.

Kwong, M. J., & Bartholomew, K. (2011). "Not just a dog": An attachment perspective on relationships with assistance dogs. *Attachment & Human Development*, *13*(5), 421–36.

Malone, H. J. (2009). Build a bridge from high school to college. *Phi Kappa Phi Forum*, *89*(3), 23.

Shaughnessy, M. F. (2008). An interview with Melissa Winkle: About assistance dogs. *Exceptional Parent*, *38*(5), 34–36.

Walker, D. A., Downey, P. M., & Cox-Henderson, J. (2010). REAL camp: A school-university collaboration to promote post-secondary educational opportunities among high school students. *The Educational Forum*, *74*(4), 297–304.

ABOUT THE AUTHORS

Kevin S. Koett, EdD, has served as a mentor, instructor, and student affairs professional in higher education for over twenty-eight years. He has served in a variety of roles at six different institutions and has been recognized for his servant-leadership as the first recipient of the Joe Buck Service Award. He holds a Bachelor of Arts in Social Studies Teaching from Augustana College (SD), a Master of Science in Higher Education Administration from Syracuse University, and a Doctorate in Educational Leadership from Morehead State University.

Carol J. Christian, EdD, has served as teacher, coach, principal, and professor in Kentucky with over thirty years of experience. She has co-authored *Privileged Thinking in Today's Schools: The Implications of Social Justice and Heart to Heart*. She was selected to serve in Kentucky's Highly Skilled Educator Program working with low-performing schools. She holds degrees from Eastern Kentucky University and a Doctorate in Education from the University of Louisville.

C. Thomas Potter II, EdD, has served the education profession as a teacher, principal, and superintendent in Kentucky for over twenty-two years. He is one of twenty-five selected superintendents to serve in a leadership cohort sponsored by the National Institute of School Leaders. He holds a Master of Arts in Secondary Education and a doctorate in Educational Administration from Morehead State University.